Horwitz, Elinor Lander
        Capital punishment, U.S.A.    Lippincott
        [c1973]
            192 p.    illus.

1. Capital punishment - Hist. — U.S.

# Capital
# Punishment, U.S.A.

# Capital Punishment, U.S.A.

**Elinor Lander Horwitz**

**J.B. Lippincott Company**
**Philadelphia and New York**

THIS BOOK IS FOR

# NORMAN

PICTURE CREDITS
PAGES 14, 19, 25, 45, 57: NEW YORK PUBLIC LIBRARY
PAGES 81, 103, 131, 154, 173: WIDE WORLD PHOTOS

**U. S. Library of Congress Cataloging in Publication Data**

Horwitz, Elinor Lander.
  Capital punishment, U. S. A.

  SUMMARY: Traces the history of capital punishment in the
United States and discusses some famous controversial criminal cases.
  1. Capital punishment—United States—History—Juvenile litera-
ture. [1. Capital punishment] I. Title.
HV8699.U5H6                    364.6'6                    72-13135
ISBN-0-397-31465-5

# Contents

# 1
## THE REPRIEVE

"I'VE BEEN THINKING about death for a long time. Now I can think about living," said Lucious Jackson, Jr., a convicted rapist who had been confined to death row in Georgia State Prison for the past three years.

His neighbor down the hall cried out to reporters, "I may be here for the rest of my life, but it's life, and no man wants to die."

"There wasn't a man in here who wasn't clapping and yelling like crazy," another prisoner added.

At the Florida State Prison Farm eighty of the ninety-seven occupants of death row returned to their cells from a movie just in time to hear the news on the radio. The response was a clamor of shouts and hoots, the rattling of cell doors, and cries of "Right on, Mr. Justices!"

The date was June 29, 1972, and across the country the condemned and their families rejoiced at the news that the Supreme Court, in a crucial and historic decision, had ruled that capital punishment—as it was administered in the United States—is unconstitutional. Lucious Jackson had been one of three defendants in the case, which was brought by the N.A.A.C.P. Legal Defense and Educational Fund aided by several religious and civil liberties groups.

In the flurry of speculation about the future, the one indisputable result of the decision was that the six hundred prisoners awaiting execution in prisons in thirty-two states were released from the death penalty. The unprecedented backlog of cases was created by a five-year moratorium on executions effected by the N.A.A.C.P. Legal Defense Fund while cases were being prepared for trial before the high court. During the moratorium, juries continued to sentence offenders to death and the number of pending executions rose from 434 in 1968 to 600 by 1972. Whether these prisoners will spend their entire lives in jail or become eligible for parole at some future date is yet to be seen. But it is now possible that José Mongé, who died in the gas chamber of a Colorado prison in June, 1967, for killing his pregnant wife and three children, will enter the annals of crime as the last man to have been legally executed in the United States.

To those whose lives depended on the decision and to many of the jurists, legislators, penologists, psychologists, and lay people who have fought for an end to capital punishment, the action of the Supreme Court was a triumph of twentieth-century enlightenment and humanitarianism. It is important to note, however, that at the time of the decision fourteen states and forty foreign nations had already either totally abolished or very severely restricted the death penalty.

The questions posed and answered by the nine justices in deciding whether or not capital punishment is unconstitutional form a scholarly evaluation of relevant cases from the past and statistical findings on the status of capital punishment in the United States today. The majority emphasized the facts that the death penalty has not been found to be an effective deterrent to crime and that it is applied very rarely and also discriminatorily. Justice Brennan compared the arbitrary dealing out of the death sentence to "a lottery system." Justice Stewart found that "If any basis can be discerned for the selection of those few to be sentenced to die, it is the constitutionally impermissible basis of race." He described the sentence of death in America today as "freakishly imposed."

"One searches our chronicles in vain for the execution of any member of the affluent strata of this society," Justice Douglas added.

In scrutinizing the Eighth Amendment prohibition on "cruel and unusual punishment"—originally intended simply to rule out torture and barbaric methods of execution—the court found that capital punishment per se has become both "cruel" and "unusual" and has proven to be "morally unacceptable to the people of the United States at this time in their history."

The four dissenting justices found no violation of constitutional guarantees and held that abolishing capital punishment is not properly the business of judges but should be decided by the states through their legislators.

The 599 men and one woman who had just been reprieved from the ruthless and irrevocable punishment of death struggled to verbalize their emotions for an eager press corps. One man posed in his cell with a dazed expression surrounded by smiling relatives. Another was photographed standing, hands on hips, alongside the electric chair in a Tennessee prison.

One inmate, asked for his reactions by a reporter, said

simply, "It was such a happy occasion that I cried." He had spent six years on death row awaiting execution for the murder of a policeman, which he insisted was "an accident." Another, a black man sentenced to death for the rape of a white woman, assured members of the press that the death penalty does not in any way serve as a deterrent to a man about to commit a crime. He added, "The death penalty is the most cruel thing on the face of the earth, especially for rape."

A number of prisoners spoke of their hopes for parole. Lucious Jackson, Jr. felt that "I got a fighting chance now of some day getting outside." Others were more pessimistic, but their parents and wives expressed faith in their ultimate release. Macabre jokes about "Old Sparky"—prison slang for the electric chair—echoed through death row corridors.

As lawyers and legislators debate possible interpretations and applications of the justices' opinions, the decision remains—whatever its consequences—a major landmark in the history of capital punishment.

Legal executions have taken place in every known society and capital punishment has been viewed throughout history as justifiable retribution, a necessary safeguard to society, and the most effective deterrent to crime. The biblical injunction "He that smiteth a man, so that he shall die, shall be surely put to death" (Exodus 21:12) has been rephrased and given top billing in legal codes all over the world. It is indicative of our primitive faith that our newspapers traditionally report executions with the confident phrases: "The prisoner paid his debt to society at 10:25 A.M." or "Justice was done at 2:03 in the afternoon."

Yet suddenly retribution and vengeance are out of date and the word "justice," as applied to capital punishment, is being written in quotes. The novelist Arthur Koestler, who narrowly escaped execution after being sentenced to death without a hearing while covering the Spanish Civil War for a British newspaper, wrote a book titled *Reflections on Hanging*. "Deep inside every civilized being there lurks a tiny Stone Age man," he warned, "screaming an eye for an eye. But we would rather not have that little fur-clad figure dictate the law of the land."

Time-honored certainties about the effectiveness of the death penalty are falling before increasingly persuasive statistics. New questions are being framed. If we believe in the sanctity of life, whether on a religious basis or on simple humanitarian grounds, we must ask whether the state, which represents all the individuals comprising it, should violate this sanctity by taking the life of any of its citizens, even its most heinous offenders. Are the laws that found approval in primitive societies morally acceptable to thoughtful people today?

The Supreme Court has answered no.

Are the law enforcement provisions, once considered liberal, that the founding fathers of *this* society believed in, immutable in today's more humane and sophisticated times?

Again, the Supreme Court has answered no.

And, quite aside from the matter of philosophy—does capital punishment *work?* Does it accomplish purposes that justify its cruelty?

The court has answered no.

# ‖
# A HISTORY
# OF CAPITAL PUNISHMENT

HOW DID WE ARRIVE at this stage in our judicial and legislative history? How did the evolution of our principles and practices lead us to the stand the Supreme Court has now taken?

The right and the duty of the state to defend itself against men and women who menace its security has been unquestioned throughout history. What has changed from era to era and from land to land is the definition of menace—and the methods of defense. Capital punishment—the legal taking of the life of a transgressor—is the most primitive and universal means of dealing with offenders against society, and in the history of this relatively young country alone, men and women have been sentenced to death for close to one hundred different crimes including theft, arson, counterfeiting, bigamy, witchcraft, and passing atomic secrets. The roster of misdeeds which in some places and at some times have carried the penalty of death—and the horrifying variety of means employed for effecting this punishment—comprises a shocking history of man's brutality to man.

The story of capital punishment goes as far back as recorded history, and there is no reason to believe that it does not extend even deeper into the past. In the earliest writing on the subject, the great code of laws drawn up by the Babylonian Hammurabi in about 2000 B.C., numerous offenses punishable by death are listed beginning with the crime of cheating people when selling them beer. The code, which was based on earlier legal precedent, recommends as means of execution burning, drowning, and impalement on sharp sticks.

Since that time citizens have taken the lives of their fellow men for both grave and trivial offenses and sometimes for no offense whatsoever. The Romans rounded up slaves and captives and killed them simply for sport. The ancient Persians punished a man by death if, while tidying up, he accidentally sat on the king's throne. In eighteenth-century England, children were hanged for stealing a piece of bread or a few pennies.

A great deal of ingenuity has been spent on devising methods for carrying out the death penalty through the ages, and lawbreakers have been hanged, beheaded, stoned, stretched on racks, pressed to death with weights, cut into pieces, disemboweled, torn to bits by horses, consumed by lions, burned alive, drowned, crucified, torn apart with red-hot pincers, shot, electrocuted, gassed.

Today we automatically think of murder as *the* capital crime, yet it is only in relatively modern times that homicide has become the most common offense to be punished by death. In early eras murder was not considered a proper concern of the state at all. If a man was killed a member of his family—designated "the avenger of the blood"—retaliated by promptly hacking up the murderer. Vendettas still go on in parts of the modern world and it was this ancient

*This primitive type of gallows was used in Anglo-Saxon times. It provided one ladder for the victim and one for the hangman.*

zest for personal revenge which led Jack Ruby, without benefit of family relationship, to see that the murder of his adored President Kennedy was "properly" repaid. In accordance with our current concepts of law and psychology he was judged to be emotionally unstable, perhaps mad, to have so usurped the right of the state. Yet older societies might have deemed him a just man.

In early Teutonic and Celtic law a practical alternative to the blood feud was adopted and a murderer was expected to atone by paying a fine. The value of each life was estimated according to the victim's age and station and his murderer gave half this sum to the victim's family and half to the king, as repayment for the loss of a valuable man. If a slave was killed, his master was recompensed. The family of the slain man, however, retained the option of taking the criminal's life rather than his money until 890 when Alfred the Great decreed that the blood feud was lawful only if the killer had refused to pay the price demanded. A man who was willing but unable to raise the purse usually went into exile or into slavery. Of course, a rich man could afford to knock off enemies with regularity, and simply pay for the privilege. More serious crimes which could not be repaid except by the death of the offender included housebreaking, arson, and betrayal of a lord.

Crimes which have been deemed "capital"—in other words, deserving of the death penalty—fall into three general categories: crimes against the person, crimes against property, and crimes which jeopardize the security of the country. Crimes against the person include such specialized types of killing as infanticide, patricide, lynching, killing in a duel, killing while committing some other crime such as robbery. Other crimes against the person include assaults which need not be fatal such as rape, kidnapping, and train wrecking. Crimes against the state include treason, collaboration with the enemy, spying, raising a rebellion or a mutiny, assault on the head of state. Economic crimes include robbery, currency speculation, counterfeiting, and many, many others. Although we do not usually think of economic crimes in relation to the death penalty, in a broad world view they have constituted by far the greatest number of offenses for which people have been sentenced to death.

Although the lists of capital crimes have varied considerably, all through history the question of who receives the death penalty and who does not has depended not only on the seriousness of the crime but on the status of the offender. In India, Brahmins, members of the highest caste, were not subject to the death penalty. In ancient Greece, the Spartans only executed slaves, but the Athenians also executed citizens when they were considered socially or morally menacing to the security of the city-state and its rulers. In colonial America there were crimes capital for slaves which were not capital if committed by free white men. In most civilizations, the means of execution has also been dictated by the social class of the condemned. Athenian citizens usually drew the sentence of banishment but slaves and other noncitizens were burned at the stake or crucified, leaving no question whatsoever about the finality of the punishment. Banishment was, however, a genuine death sentence in days when being dropped on an island or in the wilderness without weapons or food made a man easy prey to barbaric tribes and wild beasts.

One of the most famous accounts of an execution is found in Plato's dialogue called the *Phaedo.* It tells of the death of Socrates, the great Athenian philosopher, who was condemned for instilling "dangerous" ideas in the minds of the young. He was sentenced to death, but because of the great esteem in which he was held, he was offered the singular alternative of a dignified and painless self-execution. Surrounded by a select group of friends Socrates sat in his cell debating the meaning of death. When ready, he summoned the jailer who arrived with the poison cup of hemlock. The account of his death follows:

Socrates said: You, my good friend, who are experienced in these matters, shall give me directions how I am to proceed. The man answered: You have only to walk about until your legs are heavy and then to lie down, and the poison will act. At the same time he handed the cup to Socrates who, in the easiest and gentlest manner, without the least fear or change of colour or feature, looking at the man with all his eyes, took the cup and said: What do you say about making a libation out of this cup to any god? May I, or not? The man answered: We only prepare, Socrates, just so much as we deem enough. I understand, he said: but I may and must ask the gods to prosper my journey from this to the other world—even so—and so be it according to my prayer. Then raising

16

the cup to his lips, quite readily and cheerfully he drank of the poison . . . he walked about until, as he said, his legs began to fail, and then he lay on his back, according to directions, and the man who gave him the poison now and then looked at his feet and legs; and after a while he pressed his foot hard, and asked him if he could feel; and he said, No; and then his leg, and so upwards and upwards, and showed us that he was cold and stiff. And he felt them himself and said: When the poison reaches the heart, that will be the end. He was beginning to grow cold about the groin, when he uncovered his face, for he had covered himself up and said—they were his last words—he said: Crito, I owe a cock to Aesculapius; will you remember to pay the debt? The debt shall be paid, said Crito; is there anything else? There was no answer to the question; but in a minute or two a movement was heard, and the attendants uncovered him; his eyes were set, and Crito closed his eyes and mouth.

Aesculapius was the Greek god of health and Socrates believed that in crossing into the afterworld he would find eternal health. The sacrifice to the god was a final expression of thanks.

The Old Testament is constantly cited as justification for capital punishment and many references can be found to such practices as stoning, beheading, and hanging. Stoning to death by the congregation was the Mosaic punishment for several crimes including blasphemy, adultery, kidnapping, murder, incest, and the disobedience of children. The following passage appears in the 21st chapter of Leviticus:

If a man have a stubborn and rebellious son, which will not obey the voice of his father, or the voice of his mother, and that, when they have chastened him, will not hearken unto them; Then shall his father and mother lay hold on him, and bring him out unto the elders of his city, and unto the gate of his place; and they shall say unto the elders of his city, This our son is stubborn and rebellious, he will not obey our voice; he is a glutton and a drunkard. And all the men of his city shall stone him with stones, that he die; so shalt thou put evil away from among you; and all Israel shall hear, and fear.

In actual practice the Hebrew courts had so many meticulous safeguards against executing the innocent that conviction for certain crimes became almost impossible. To condemn a man to death on a charge of murder two eyewitnesses were required to submit their testimony. A witness found to have given false evidence in a capital crime was punished by receiving the form of execution which would have been administered to the accused.

Beheading was a popular means of execution in Egypt and Assyria and it continued in vogue in western Europe until the end of the eighteenth century and into the twentieth in the east. In the Far East a sword or cleaver is used and in the Near East a scimitar. Beheading is closely related to the primitive custom of maiming—of removing the offending part of the body. A man who stole, in many societies, had a hand cut off; a sexual offender might be castrated; a man who cursed God ran the risk of losing his tongue. Removal of the head, of course, presents a crucial difference but it can be viewed as the maiming method of dealing with people who have wicked thoughts and plot wicked deeds. It has also always been considered a relatively humane method of execution particularly when effected by the guillotine, which is still used in France today.

The Romans learned beheading and crucifixion from their neighbors and they invented a few novelties of their own as well. They added to the list of capital crimes such

*A nineteenth-century Chinese executioner carries the tool of his trade.*

offenses as disturbing the peace at night, publishing libels, and singing insulting songs. Vestal virgins, assigned to holy rituals in the temples, were buried alive if found to be unchaste. Other wrongdoers were hurled from rocky ledges, impaled on sharp sticks, or crucified.

At the time of the death of Jesus of Nazareth, crucifixion, which had a long history in Assyria, Egypt, Persia, Carthage, and Greece, was considered the most humiliating means of putting a man to death. It was reserved for slaves and particularly contemptible criminals. The crucified man, suffering agonies from thirst, hunger, and exposure for as long as three days, was watched and taunted by sadistic crowds. A variation of technique involved hanging a man upside down and, although this was considered even more degrading, it resulted in a rapid and merciful lapse into unconsciousness. The Emperor Constantine abolished crucifixion in the Roman Empire in the fourth century A.D., but it remained in favor many years later in Europe and in Japan.

A new method of execution was invented by the Romans

especially for parricides—those who murdered either or both parents. The condemned would be thrown into a sack with a wild dog, a fighting cock, a poisonous snake, and a monkey. The sack was tightly sewn and then tossed into the water. As the drowning animals attacked the drowning man justice was satisfied.

Executions also became recreational events which took place, appropriately, in the arena. The Emperor Claudius had nineteen thousand men brought to Rome to be killed in the circus as part of the entertainment. Many had committed no crime whatsoever except that of having been born into the wrong class of society. Agrippa is charged with sacrificing fourteen thousand in the arenas during his reign. The execution events featured men being speared to death and eaten by lions. Caligula delighted in mass beheadings as curtain raisers at the public games. Headsmen competed for attention with free-form decapitations, where no block was used and skill in hitting the mark could be fully appreciated. The ancient Persians had a different method of ridding themselves of criminals. The accused man was tied firmly in a boat and his body smeared with honey. The boat was set adrift and the victim would literally be eaten alive by insects over a period of days.

The first record of capital punishment in Britain dates from 450 B.C. when condemned criminals were tossed into quagmires to drown. From there it was on to throwing them into dungeons to starve and then beating and stoning to death, hanging, beheading, burning alive, and all the other fads popular on the continent. By the thirteenth century capital punishment was liberally dealt out to those people convicted of treason and numerous other crimes against person and property, which included thefts of more than a shilling.

Capital punishment in all lands was public. The intent was always to deter others from wrongdoing. In the first century the Roman historian Seneca wrote, "The more public the punishments are, the greater effect they will produce on the reformation of others." It is a fascinating fact of history that this view has been restated in virtually every known tongue and remained a completely unchallenged conviction until the end of the eighteenth century.

It was during the Middle Ages in western Europe that the most cruel and inhumane methods of death by torture became common practice. Execution for treason and for many other crimes was frequently carried out in a horrifyingly sadistic manner. Breaking a man's bones, one by one, while he was chained to a huge wheel was particularly favored in France and Germany. The British preferred drawing and quartering, which was legalized in the thirteenth century and first tried out on an unfortunate man named William Maurice, who was convicted of piracy. Capital punishment was extended to heretics, who were usually burned alive at the stake. Flaying alive was considered just punishment as was boiling a man in a huge caldron of water or oil. Molten lead was poured into wounds and special offenders were pulled to pieces by four horses, to whom their arms and legs were chained. Until comparatively recent times the wording of the sentence for high treason in England remained grimly explicit:

> That the traitor is to be taken from prison and laid on a hurdle and drawn to the gallows, then hanged by the neck until nearly dead, then cut down. Then his entrails to be cut out of his body and burnt by the executioner, then his head to be cut off, his body divided into four quarters, and afterwards set up in some open place as directed.

21

One of the most famous executioners in English history was nicknamed William Boilman. It was he who discovered that if the quarters of an executed man were boiled they resisted weather and deterioration when put on exhibition. The British have always enjoyed their historic figures in the field and four executioners, including Boilman, are enshrined in their *Dictionary of National Biography*.

For many centuries a trip around the lovely English countryside was marked by ghastly sights. The hanged were left dangling from trees and quarters and heads were displayed at crossroads, entrances into cities, and on bridges—as warnings of the fate of those who threatened the power of the Crown.

Drawing and quartering appear to have been reserved exclusively for men. Women accused of high treason went to the stake instead. Surprisingly in these brutal times, it was considered an offense to modesty to dissect a living female. The eighteenth-century English jurist Sir William Blackstone explained the problem in his *Commentaries on the Laws of England.* He wrote, matter-of-factly, that women were burned because of "the decency due to sex which forbids exposing and publicly mangling their bodies."

For a great variety of offenses beheading was an upper-class privilege, with hanging the method of execution of the common man. Barons often held the privilege of dealing with traitors directly and most kept both a gallows and a drowning pit handy on the grounds.

Educated citizens might be spared the death sentence for felonies by the intercession of the church. At first only clerics, and later all men who could read, were judged by the more merciful ecclesiastical courts rather than the civil courts. The fifty-first psalm was assigned to be read aloud as a literacy test, and it became known, with grim humor, as "the neck verse." Clerical immunity or "benefit of clergy" was granted only for a first offense after 1487 and to avoid the problem of repeaters, a brand was put on the left thumb of a pardoned criminal for identification. The Elizabethan poet Ben Jonson killed an actor in a duel and was spared the death sentence by a clerical court. He bore an M—for murder—branded on his hand for the rest of his life.

The number of men and women who have been tortured and killed throughout the world in the name of God cannot possibly be counted. In Europe beginning in the Middle Ages, the common sentence for witchcraft was drowning or burning. Joan of Arc was burned at the stake in the fifteenth century after judgment was passed by a French ecclesiastical court. During many years of the Spanish Inquisition, which extended from the fourteenth into the nineteenth century, mass burnings speeded up the eradication of accused heretics. Executions were often preceded by torture, which usually succeeded in the aim of drawing a confession from the condemned man or woman. Confession was important because if a heretic died without pleading guilty his estate went to his family. Admission of guilt meant that all his money and goods reverted to the state, and this source of revenue was closely guarded. One of the common means of torture was pressing, in which the subject was chained to the floor while increasingly heavy weights were laid on his body. If confession was required, care was taken not to collapse the rib cage which would cause death. If confession was obtained, the condemned man or woman might be released from the weights and carted off to the stake, or simply killed with added weights.

Something new was added to the annals of justice when a British Admiralty law of 1450 made stealing a rope, a net, or cords of a value of nine pence punishable by death. The culprit was to be bound hand and foot. His throat was to be cut and his tongue pulled out. What remained was to be thrown in the sea in the best naval tradition.

One extraordinary sidelight on capital punishment was the practice of executing animals who killed human beings. This strange custom, which could surely not be justified as a deterrence to other criminally inclined beasts, began in the Middle Ages. The last recorded case concerned a dog who participated in some fashion in a robbery and murder in Switzerland in 1906! The procedure in animal executions was perfectly fair by the standards of the day. The creature would be assigned counsel to defend him during his trial since he could not defend himself. Evidence was to be presented in accordance with the rules of the court. If the accused was found guilty, sentence would be passed, with hanging the usual method of execution. A French sow, convicted of killing a baby, was publicly hanged in 1386. A few years later a horse who kicked his master to death was hanged in Dijon, although testimony that the man provoked the horse had been brought out in court. In 1750 a man and a donkey were tried together. The man's crime was having sexual intercourse with the animal and both were to be burned alive at the same stake. The man was so executed, but in an unprecedented decision, the animal was spared. A parish priest and other leading citizens of the town testified that the beast was of good character, had been the victim of the man's immorality, and had not committed the act of her own free will.

In England the reign of Henry VIII was marked by unprecedented numbers of executions. It is recorded that seventy-two thousand people were hanged and a good many others beheaded. The great humanist, Sir Thomas More,

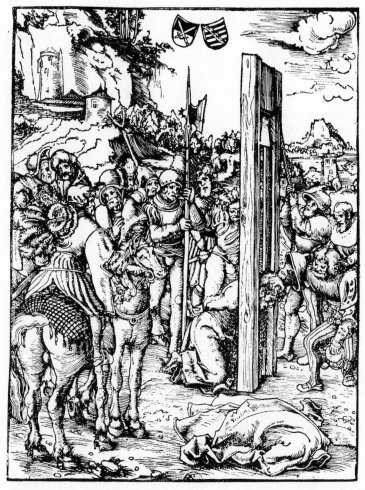

*This sixteenth-century engraving shows a mechanical device which was used for beheadings in Germany two hundred years before the invention of the guillotine.*

spoke out against capital punishment in his *Utopia*, a book which described an imaginary ideal society. He was be-headed for opposing the king's divorce and his head was displayed on London Bridge. Henry was the monarch who legalized the new idea of boiling people in man-sized pots, but it seems to have been reserved for special cases. A huge caldron mounted on a strong iron tripod was placed over burning logs: Heat to a boil and insert prisoner. Several kitchen servants accused of poisoning their masters were cooked to death, which perhaps seemed appropriate. In 1547 Henry repealed this alternate method of execution which had been on the books for sixteen years. Rare instances of boiling alive continued to occur, however, in France as well as in England.

Hanging and beheading were the general rule, and free-form beheading gave way to use of the block in most instances. Charles I, who died with great dignity, was executed on a high block. The poet Andrew Marvell described in verse his gracious manner as he kneeled and "laid his comely head/Down, as upon a bed." The low block required the prisoner to stretch out prone on the scaffold. This was not only a degrading position to assume before the public, but it also permitted the executioner's assistants, who removed collars and held long hair out of the way of the axe, to sit on the condemned man and restrain him if he threatened a struggle. This sort of behavior was not expected of the higher class of people. (The expectation seems to have persisted. In a hearing before the Royal Commission on Capital Punishment during the 1960's, the last official British executioner reported that he had never witnessed unseemly behavior at the gallows by *any* of Her Majesty's subjects. He did, however, tell a shameful story of a spy from another country who "kicked up rough" and had to be restrained. "I personally have noticed that English people take their punishment better than foreigners," he said with satisfaction.)

One famous Englishman who was also noted for his gentlemanly behavior at the scaffold was Sir Walter Raleigh, who was executed in the reign of James I on flimsy evidence of involvement in a treasonous plot. It is reported that he asked to see the headsman's axe, admired the keenness of the blade, and commented with bitter wit, " 'Tis a sharp medicine, but it will cure all diseases."

Beheading was classier than hanging and the high block more chic than the low block, but the most posh method of all for an Englishman was to be decapitated by a sword rather than by an axe. When Henry VIII sentenced his wife Anne Boleyn to death, he wanted everything carried off in style. He sent a delegation to France where a noted executioner was in residence in the handy city of Calais, directly across the channel. The Frenchman, whose name was Rombaud, invited the English investigators to watch a demonstration of his skill. Two men, who had been involved in the same crime, were to be executed together. Rombaud had the prisoners tied to chairs, which were placed facing each other with a space of several feet separating them. Taking a position between the two men, the executioner raised his gleaming double-edged sword and swung it around once in an arc, severing both heads on the way. The English delegation was impressed. When the beautiful young English queen was beheaded by Rombaud soon afterward in an elegant free-form swing the crowd was thrilled.

In a spirit of humane concern, the French replaced their famous executioners with the even more efficient machine known as the guillotine in 1789. Dr. Joseph Guillotin, for whom the beheading contraption was named, was a deputy to the National Assembly in Paris, who pushed legislation which made the invention the only legal method of execution in France. At first it was called the "Louisiette" after its designer, Dr. Antoine Louise, but the name didn't stick. The contract had been let to the lowest bidder, a meticulous German harpsichord maker named Tobias Schmidt, who built the first guillotine and tried it out on live sheep and next on human corpses before he was satisfied that it was perfect. When the first man was executed by the new machine the audience was dismayed. A newspaper of the day reported that the whole thing was over so quickly that the people cried out for the return of the showy headsman and the good old gallows.

Nonetheless, the guillotine caught on. It was not the first mechanical device which utilized a heavy blade dropped ten or twelve feet along metal runners. It was simply the most efficient. The Scottish had a primitive fascimile called "The Maiden" in the sixteenth century, and in the fourteenth century the so-called "Halifax Gibbet" accomplished the same purpose. The guillotine worked so neatly that it became popular in Germany as well. Sweden and Denmark, however, stayed loyal to the axe and Spain and Austria to the garotte—an iron collar that killed by slow strangulation. During the Reign of Terror, following the French Revolution, 1,250 people were beheaded in thirteen months on a guillotine permanently stationed in the Place de la Révolution. When shopkeepers in the neighborhood complained that the crowds watching the beheadings made it impossible for people to get to their shops it was moved to another site where almost 2,000 men and women were slain in under two months. Even at the guillotine, the parricide was singled out for special shame. He was led to his death barefoot and veiled in black.

Toy guillotines were sold at the scaffold and were often accompanied by a small cage filled with live sparrows or mice. They became the best-selling toys of the period and nurseries in the homes of the wealthy became scenes of grisly merriment.

An eighteenth-century Swedish code lists sixty-eight capital crimes and recommends decapitation for murder, blasphemy, sorcery, arson, treason, adultery, and conspiracy, and decapitation followed by public burning of the body for sodomy, poisoning, and cases of sorcery followed by the death of the bewitched. For crimes such as infanticide and murder by a servant of his master, decapitation was to be preceded by chopping off the right hand. The explanation was that God so willed and if His will was not carried out He would send plagues and famine as expression of His anger and wipe out everyone in the land in revenge against a single unpunished criminal.

In England transportation became one alternative to execution and starting in the seventeenth century, but particularly after the Transportation Act of 1717, large numbers of felons were shipped to the colonies. A great number of people in our present white population are descended from these relocated prisoners.

The high point in sheer numbers of capital crimes was reached in England in the late eighteenth and early nineteenth century. In the fifteenth century there were only eight capital crimes, the most serious of which was considered to be treason. The seven others were petty treason, murder, larceny, robbery, burglary, rape, and arson. By the end of the seventeenth century almost 50 capital crimes were listed in the legal codes. Dozens were added under the reigns of George II and George III. Blackstone counted 160 in 1769. The number was to rise to 240 within a few decades: crimes against the state, against person, against property, and against the public peace. They ranged in severity from robbing a rabbit warren or fishing in a private pond to murdering the king. Other capital crimes included stealing forty shillings from a dwelling or five from a shop, associating with gypsies, writing threatening letters, or impersonating a Greenwich pensioner. Children of eight and ten struggled to mount the high steps to the scaffold with their short legs, where they were hanged for theft, arson, and other offenses against property. One tiny girl was so light that when the drop opened she dangled from the rope unharmed.

When a man was convicted of a capital offense all his money and property were forfeited to the state and his family was denied any right of inheritance. This was the law whether he was actually executed or not. He was not allowed to testify in his own behalf or confront those who testified against him. He was not permitted counsel. Hanging was the commonest mode of execution but a woman who killed her husband—a crime known as petty treason—was burned at the stake. Huge raucous crowds drank and reveled in the most bestial manner at the scaffold, where pickpockets thronged, although picking pockets was a capital offense and had been for three hundred years. Guidebooks used the permanent gallows, which were the commonest tall features of the towns and countryside, as landmarks. "Turn right at the gallows," was the way to find the church. A left by the gibbet would take you to the windmill, where a right turn led to the next town, whose gallows could be spotted as you mounted the hill.

It was against this violent western European background —in particular the practices of seventeenth- and eighteenth-century England—that the American colonies codified their own views of capital punishment. The precedents they accepted and those they rejected shaped the early criminal code of this country.

# COLONISTS, WITCHES,
# AND THE BILL OF RIGHTS

WHEN THE SUPREME COURT RULED against capital punishment in 1972, the United States was the major advocate of
the death penalty among the advanced nations of the
world. This fact, which outrages American opponents of
capital punishment, is both shocking and ironic because the
early colonists were strikingly ahead of their time in their
commitment to the humanization of the criminal laws.

What may seem to us harsh punishments compared with
those of the twentieth century were extraordinarily liberal
compared to seventeenth-century practices in the mother
country and in most of the other nations of the world. Every
schoolchild knows that the stern Puritans flung lawbreakers
into stocks and often flogged thieves in the public square.
What is less well known is that, during this period, the theft
of five shillings was punishable by hanging in England. The
Puritans considered the fact that the American Indians
burned captives at the stake proof of their savagery, but
burning alive was only one of the sadistic torture-deaths
readily available in many "civilized" European societies.

There is no question that the colonists deemed the death

31

penalty a necessity, but they radically circumscribed its scope. The average number of capital crimes in each colony was about twelve, although there was considerable diversity. Furthermore, execution in America was usually accomplished in swift and merciful fashion. With some exceptions —a few slaves burned at the stake and one incident of pressing—the only authorized method of execution in this country until the end of the nineteenth century was hanging, which was considered the most humane. Shooting was reserved under martial laws for spies, traitors, and deserters. Commonplace European practices such as drawing and quartering, disemboweling, and burning alive were regarded with the greatest possible disapproval.

Most of the original colonies executed culprits found guilty of murder, treason, counterfeiting, horse theft, arson, robbery, rape, sodomy, and exciting slaves to rebellion. Executing men was wasteful in the new underpopulated country where all hands were needed, but the total inadequacy of the jails made it necessary to hang those offenders who were considered a serious threat to society.

English common law guided legal thought and procedure in the colonies and its influence was particularly marked in the criminal code of New York. The laws of Massachusetts and Connecticut, however, seem more biblical than British in their inspiration. A 1690 penal code in the Connecticut Colony read:

> If any man shall have or worship any other God but the true God, he shall be put to death.
>
> If any man or woman be a witch, that is, hath or consulteth with a familiar spirit, he or she shall be put to death.
>
> If any man stealeth a man or mankind, he shall be put to death.

> If any child or children above sixteen years and of sufficient understanding shall curse or smite father or mother, he shall be put to death.

> If any man have a stubborn and rebellious son of sufficient years and understanding, viz: sixteen years of age who will not obey the voice of his father or the voice of his mother, and when they have chastened him will not hearken unto them; then may his father and his mother lay hold of him and bring him to the magistrates assembled at court and testify unto them, and such a son shall be put to death.

An English woman who visited the colony a few years later wrote of the trial of a nineteen-year-old girl brought to court by her parents, both of whom swore against her under the last of these laws. The judges, after careful consideration of the charges of "stubbornness" and "rebelliousness," cited not the English law but Deuteronomy 21:20 and decreed that the punishment only applied to sons. There is no evidence that this law was ever actually carried out in Connecticut.

Lack of uniformity was the rule in the early days. In Virginia the penal code listed seventy capital crimes for which Negro slaves could be executed and only five for whites. North Carolina had a severe criminal code which included all the usual capital offenses as well as concealing a slave with intent to free him, taking a free Negro out of the state for purposes of selling him into slavery, circulating seditious literature among slaves, dueling if a death occurred, statutory rape, and second-offense forgery. Because there were no adequate prisons in the state these early laws remained in force until 1837.

The Commonwealth of Pennsylvania and the Massachusetts Bay Colony represent the two poles of leniency and severity. The Quaker influence in Pennsylvania resulted in the country's most humane law and the Puritan presence in Massachusetts led to its sternest.

William Penn's Great Act of 1682 actually succeeded in confining the death penalty in Pennsylvania to only two crimes—murder and treason. This extraordinarily modern piece of legislation lasted only a short time but, while it did, the Commonwealth of Pennsylvania was referred to contemptuously by legislators in England as "Ye greatest refuge and shelter for pirates and rogues in America."

In 1701 the Newcastle Code was enacted which prescribed flogging and mutilations for offenses which, in other colonies, were capital crimes. Castration was one of the permissible punishments and it could be performed on three grounds: second-offense rape, sodomy, or bestiality. When news of this new law reached the English Privy Council they objected strenuously. Although the current criminal code of England was almost incredibly brutal, the council was aghast at the decision of the gentle Quakers. Castration, they said, was simply not done in England and was certainly most unseemly in the colonies. There are no records which indicate whether this provision of the code was ever carried out in practice. We do know that at this time blacks were tried by special courts and were liable to execution for burglary and first-offense rape in addition to the general laws pertaining to murder and treason. If slaves were executed their masters were reimbursed for their appraised value with funds from the public treasury.

By 1718 the lenient laws of William Penn had been overruled by the Crown and thirteen crimes became punishable by death: treason, murder, manslaughter by stabbing, serious maiming, burglary, arson, highway robbery, buggery, sodomy, rape, concealing the death of a bastard child, ad-

34

vising on the killing of such an infant, and witchcraft. Later Pennsylvania again took a lead in humanitarian reform when it became the center of the early abolition movement. In 1834 it was the first state to rule out public hangings. Records kept from 1682 until that date show a total of 252 executions—less than two a year—about half of them for murder. Twenty-one of those executed were women.

It was law throughout the country that if a woman condemned to death could prove that she was pregnant execution would be canceled. A female burglar from New York who had been sentenced to hang appears in the early annals of crime in America. It is reported that "the prisoner pleaded her belly." A special jury of women was impaneled and conducted a thorough examination. Finding her "quick with child" they ordered that she be reprieved.

Hangings were public attractions in this country, as they were throughout the world. The condemned man rode to the gallows in a wagon, often seated on his coffin. Sometimes he walked behind the wagon and his relatives strode alongside. His hands were tied and he frequently wore the rope around his neck. The most primitive type of gallows was a "hanging tree." A ladder was placed against the trunk and the prisoner and hangman climbed it together. The executioner tossed the rope over a strong limb, took a firm grip and pushed the victim off the ladder. A more common method was to stand the prisoner on the cart while the rope was adjusted around the limb. At the hangman's signal the driver moved the cart and the man was left dangling. Both methods often resulted in agonizing deaths from slow strangulation.

When gallows were constructed the device of the drop was employed. This was a simple collapsible trapdoor or platform. As the latch was sprung the prisoner's neck was

35

broken by the sudden fall and death was instantaneous. Skillful hangmen could ascertain the exact height required by consideration of the prisoner's build and weight. Too short a drop would not break the neck. Too long a drop could result in the ghastly possibility of the victim's head being torn off. An assistant was posted below to pull on the man's legs if he appeared to be struggling.

The most notorious episode in the early history of capital punishment in this country was the witchcraft delusion which took place in Salem, Massachusetts, in 1692. In one year twenty men and women were put to death. The laws in the Massachusetts Bay Colony were the first written document on capital punishment drawn up in this country. Titled "The Capitall Lawes of New England" and dated 1636 they made punishable by death: idolatry, withcraft, blasphemy, murder, assault in sudden anger, adultery, rape, statutory rape, sodomy, buggery, man-stealing, rebellion, and perjury in a capital crime. Not English law, but Old Testament authority was cited. A biblical quotation followed each law.

As to witchcraft—virtually everyone of the period believed in it. During the sixteenth and seventeenth centuries an estimated two hundred thousand people were hanged, burned alive, or drowned for the crime in Europe. Nine hundred witches were burned in the seventeenth century in the city of Bamberg alone. Witches were hanged in England and New England but on the continent of Europe they were traditionally burned alive. In countries where witchcraft was considered heresy, not merely a felony, the idea seems to have been that burning prevented resurrection. In many cases the victim was not actually burned alive but was sympathetically strangled to death by the executioner before the flames reached the body.

When the Salem panic occurred there had been a recent epidemic of witchcraft hysteria in England in the 1640's and a few executions for witchcraft had already taken place in the colonies. A witch had been hanged in Charlestown in 1648, another in Boston in 1655. When suddenly, in Salem Village, Massachusetts, a group of young girls gave every evidence of having been bewitched there was panic in the community. The religious men and women of the colony were familiar with witchcraft from their Bible-reading and they paid particular heed to the injunction, "Thou shalt not suffer a witch to live." There was a firm prevailing belief in demons and magic and the ability and desire of the Devil to overcome the powers of good. Even Isaac Newton believed in witches and carried charms to ward them off. Not only biblical law but European canon law and civil law had prescribed death for witches ever since the fifteenth century. An Inquisitor's Manual, written in 1489, gave valuable advice to inquisitors on the questions to ask men and women under torture which would lead to "voluntary" confessions of witchcraft. In the sixteenth century French scholars argued about the number of demons and infernal princes who served Satan. The most respected count was 7,409,127.

The witchcraft delusion which took place in Salem Village—now the township of Danvers but then part of Salem —began when ten girls aged nine to seventeen started meeting together in the kitchen of the minister's house to listen to stories told by the Reverend Parris's West Indian slave, Tituba. Tituba, who had been converted to Christianity but had grown up steeped in the secrets of voodoo, magic, and fortune-telling, fascinated the girls with her talk of spells and mystery. She taught them palm reading and told them bloodcurdling tales of secret forces at work in the world. In the stern God-fearing society in which they lived the girls

37

would probably have been punished for encouraging these tales and they were cautious and secretive about their get-togethers.

Two of them were servants in prominent homes and the youngest, little Elizabeth Parris, was the minister's own daughter. It was she who awakened in the middle of one night in a frenzy. Perhaps her fear of punishment disturbed her sleep or it may be that Tituba's tales brought on nightmares. All we know is that the child screamed with terror, seemed to see dreadful creatures filling the corners of the room, refused consolation, and the next day would not eat. Her anxious parents called the doctor who came over at once. He examined the hysterical child with great care and announced his diagnosis. Her affliction, he said, was the obvious result of witchcraft. He had seen such cases and there was no doubt in his mind. Someone in the village, he said, had cast an evil spell on the poor child.

It was of the greatest importance that the villagers discover who had sent these torments to Elizabeth because, as everyone knew, the whole village might be wiped out if the witch was not hunted out and destroyed. It was an undisputed fact that witches not only harmed, and even killed, men and women but could also cast spells which would slay valuable farm animals and destroy an entire year's harvest.

News spread through the town and as the children who had been involved in the meetings with Tituba heard of Elizabeth's seizures they began to scream and shout, roll on the floor, run from invisible creatures who were pinching and biting them. First one girl and then another was seized with spasms of writhing. The villagers looked on with horror as children they'd known all their lives suddenly appeared to have fallen into a state of total madness. One of the girls who worked as a kitchen maid was severely spanked by her master, who told anyone who would listen that she seemed much the better for the punishment. But few heeded him. Instead, the girls were pressed to identify the witch—and they did. They named three at first: Tituba, Goodwife Osburn, and Sarah Goode. Four village officials signed complaints against the three women and the mad disastrous witch hunt was on.

Did the girls, who certainly believed in witchcraft, actually delude themselves into thinking they were bewitched or did they simply pretend? What seems to have started as thoughtless attention-seeking developed into calamitous hysteria. At the trials, which were held in prescribed legal fashion, the suspected witches were accused by stern colonial magistrates and then questioned. There were virtually no lawyers in the country and there was no tradition of a legal defense. The court sought confession and tried, by inquiry, to lead the women to acknowledge that they had signed a pact with the Devil and had inscribed the Devil's book, in which were written the names of all those who served him.

If the defendant remembered, under questioning, a dream in which she was pursued by strange unidentifiable creatures, that was a sure sign. If she kept a doll it was obvious that she had fashioned it as an image of someone she wished to torment or kill. The usual method of extracting confessions from witches in Europe was by torture, but in Salem this was not permitted with one notable exception. The procedure was simply a matter of asking enough questions: What malicious things had she said about others? Did anyone remember thinking her odd? What exactly was the matter with her cow, the one who was ailing? Did anyone know for sure what had caused her husband's death five years before?

Accepted incriminating testimony against the suspects was so-called "spectral evidence" which simply meant that one of the afflicted girls could testify to having seen the witch's "spectre"—an apparition or image which appeared to the victim either while awake or in a dream, and tormented her.

Scores of women and several men were accused as the trials went on. The girls were present in the courtroom where they created great confusion by convulsing on the floor, screaming, biting at their arms, rolling their eyes, and carrying on in the most theatrical style imaginable. When the din totally interrupted the proceedings, the suspected witch would be ordered to touch the girls and "take back" the spell for a short time. It seemed to work and, so, was further evidence of the validity of the charge of witchcraft.

One of the accused was little Dorcas Goode, aged five, who readily admitted to being a witch and said she had a black snake which she kept as a familiar spirit. Dorcas was to spend eight months in jail in the heavy chains that were considered necessary to restrain the witch from casting her evil about. Her mother, who was one of the first accused, would be hanged. Tituba also confessed to witchcraft with great good cheer and told vivid stories about an imaginary yellow bird the Devil had given to her. She was jailed but not executed. A number of other suspects confessed to witchcraft—whether out of fear or unrelated guilt or because they were half-mad themselves and became convinced that they *did* have evil powers. If you firmly believed in the existence of witchcraft and if you had wished someone ill who then died of unknown causes and if you had strange dreams and once in a while thought you heard a voice calling your name, it was quite possible to begin sensing evil powers within yourself.

One of the girls, Mary Warren, cried out a confession that it was all pretense, as the horror of what was happening awakened her conscience. But at once the others accused her of witchcraft and testified to seeing her spectre—and she took it back. No one believed her confession in any case. Her supernatural affliction had already been legally proven.

Ironically, in the end all those who were hanged had insisted on their innocence and, although some died in jail, none who confessed were executed. By September of 1692 twenty men and women had died—nineteen of them by hanging. Among them was the saintly Rebecca Nurse, loved by everyone in town. Sarah Goode, when called upon by the minister to confess as she stood at the gallows, shouted, "I am no more a witch than you are a wizard and if you take away my life God will give you blood to drink." Her words raised the first doubts in the villagers' minds. Soon after, a man accused of being a wizard recited the Lord's Prayer without a pause as the noose was being adjusted. It was believed that witches chanted the prayer backwards at the witches' Sabbath and that, therefore, they hesitated, forgot, and mixed up words if asked to recite it correctly. The townspeople became increasingly uneasy. They spoke in hushed awe of the death of eighty-year-old Giles Corey, the only victim of death by pressing in the history of this country. Corey was a strange martyr. He believed in evil spirits and had originally accused his wife of witchcraft. But when he himself was accused his outrage was so great that he decided to protest. Under the law of England a defendant was given three chances to plead and a man who refused to answer to the indictment by pleading either guilty or not guilty could not be tried. Corey remained resolutely silent. From the minute he entered court he became totally mute. By order of the judges he was stretched on the floor of the jail and weights were put on his body. He took two days to die and, despite his agony, he never spoke. Arthur Miller, in his play *The Crucible*, written during the "witch hunt" of the 1950's, took as his central concern the confession of guilt and the problem of conscience. The drama centers on the victims of Salem's witch hunt and the death of Giles Corey is related to the hero, John Proctor, who is languishing in jail waiting to be hanged. He is told that Giles is dead.

PROCTOR: When were he hanged?

ELIZABETH: He were not hanged. He would not answer aye or nay to his indictment; for if he denied the charge they'd hang him surely and auction out his property . . . so he stand mute, and died Christian under the law. And so his sons will have his farm. It is the law, for he could not be condemned a wizard without he answer the indictment, aye or nay.

PROCTOR: Then how does he die?

ELIZABETH: They press him, John.

PROCTOR: Press?

ELIZABETH: Great stones they lay upon his chest until he plead aye or nay. They say he give them but two words. "More weight" he says, and died.

PROCTOR: "More weight."

ELIZABETH: Aye. It were a fearsome man, Giles Corey.

The same story with a slightly different tinge of opinion about Corey's character is told in a ballad written in 1692, probably by people who actually had known Corey.

Giles Corey was a Wizzard strong,
    A stubborn Wretch was he,

And fitt was he to hang on high
    Upon ye Locust Tree

So when before ye magistrates
    For Tryall he did come,
He would no true Confession make
    But was compleatlie dumbe.

"Giles Corey," said ye Magistrates,
    "What hast thou hearde to pleade,
To those who now accuse thy soule
    Of Crymes and horrid Deed?"

Giles Corey he sayde not a Word,
    No single Word spake he;
"Giles Corey," sayeth ye Magistrates,
    "We'll press it out of thee!"

They got them then a heavy Beam
    They layde it on his Breast,
They loaded it with heavy Stones,
    And hard upon him presst.

"More weight!" now sayde this wretched Man,
    "More weight" again he cryde,
And he did no Confession make
    But wickedly, he dyed.

After September the witch delusion died out. The people of Salem anxiously asked themselves and each other if it was possible that innocent people had been hanged. The girls continued their hysterical display and people ignored them. One of them, Anne Putnam, had her confession of guilt read from the pulpit several years later. She repented accusing the guiltless, blaming "a great delusion of Satan that deceived me." Judges and jurors, for the first time in history, admitted publicly that they had been wrong, when the people turned against them. All twelve jurymen signed a notice saying that they had been "under the power of a strong and general delusion." For many years a day of fasting and repentance was held in the town. In 1905 the Massachusetts legislature formally cleared six of the hanged "witches" of all charges.

The shameful and tragic Salem witchcraft delusion was like an epidemic which died out and never returned. The theocratic rule in Massachusetts was broken and there is not a single example of an execution for witchcraft in New England thereafter, although in England there were executions for twelve more years. In 1723 the English and Scottish laws prescribing death for witchcraft were repealed. Executions continued until 1745 in France and until the end of the century in Germany, Spain, Switzerland, and Poland. During the nineteenth century there were a number of witch burnings in South America. But all these were isolated cases. The last time an entire community rose to battle the forces of Satan which they feared would destroy them was in 1692 in Salem Village.

Executions for more commonplace capital offenses continued and only the most progressive thinkers spoke of total abolition. In England the number of people actually executed for their crimes was sharply reduced by the custom of permitting first offenders the benefit of clergy—trial by a clerical court which mercifully suspended the death sentence. This practice was more restricted in America but occurred to some degree in all colonies except Connecticut. Precautions were taken to make certain that a man could not receive this privilege twice. Branding—to mark a man's first offense—was common and might be accompanied by having an ear cut off. The brand was often applied to the forehead or cheek and, along with ear cropping, left the felon painfully disfigured, stigmatized, and readily iden-

*A horse thief is executed in Massachusetts during the Revolutionary War period. Note the coffin which has been brought along in the cart with the prisoner.*

tifiable. Both ear cropping and branding were the practice in England as well and a famous case concerns a distinguished lawyer who was accused of libel. He was branded on the cheek and had both ears cropped in addition to being imprisoned and disbarred. He was later reinstated, his guilt revoked, and he was granted indemnity and a jug of ale at three-hour intervals "to refoculate his wasted spirits." Literate males who had not committed any previous offense were granted benefit of clergy in Massachusetts for bigamy and manslaughter, counterfeiting and burglary, and the laws varied from colony to colony and later from state to state. The literacy test was later dropped and a few clergyable offenses remained on the books, if rarely in practice, until the nineteenth century.

During the eighteenth century the laws of the individual colonies became more alike. Young men sent abroad to be trained in English legal traditions upheld common law principles in the colonial legislatures and in the courts. When Blackstone's *Commentaries* was published in 1765 America bought 2,500 copies—more than were sold in England. Some famous lawyers were home-bred, however. Patrick Henry read law for six weeks in Virginia and was admitted to the bar. Alexander Hamilton persevered for four months before seeking accreditation. After the Revolutionary War the states cast off many of the outmoded aspects of the English common law and retained those that conformed to the contemporary needs of the new nation.

When the Eighth Amendment to the Constitution, prohibiting "cruel and unusual punishments," was passed in 1791 its words were precisely copied from Virginia's Declaration of Rights of 1776. Patrick Henry had spoken for the provision citing the fact that the colonists were distinguished because "they would not admit of tortures or cruel and barbarous punishment." He was fearful that without such specific prohibition the brutal practices then current in France, Spain, and Germany of extorting confessions of crime by torture might find favor at some future time in America. Similar clauses had been written into the Delaware Declaration of Rights, the Massachusetts Declaration of Rights, and the New Hampshire Bill of Rights.

There is no indication that the amendment, when written, was intended to outlaw capital punishment itself. And yet, abolitionist currents were already in the air and the history of the next two centuries was to be one of gradual narrowing and restriction of the death penalty.

# III
# REFORM AND ABOLITION

THE HISTORY OF CAPITAL PUNISHMENT in the nineteenth and twentieth centuries is that of reform and gradual abolition. Refusal to permit barbaric methods of execution was already an established and honored tradition in the new republic. Other reforms which began in the United States and spread to foreign nations were privacy of executions, a more precise definition of the crime of murder, and the right of juries to grant imprisonment rather than execution for capital crimes. Starting with the elimination of the death penalty for offenses against property, the list of capital crimes would be pared to the point where it became a rare sentence except for first-degree murder, and a number of states would totally abolish capital punishment either permanently or temporarily.

In the search for more humane methods of execution, Americans would contribute two new devices to the grisly diversity of death-dealing mechanisms which had been developed over the ages: the electric chair, adopted after a

47

botched first try in 1890, and killing by means of cyanide gas in 1924.

Although George Fox, the founder of the Quakers, preached against capital punishment as far back as the seventeenth century, the first voice to be heard loud and clear in this country and in Europe was that of an Italian jurist named Cesare Beccaria. His book, *On Crimes and Punishments*, published at the end of the eighteenth century, fired idealists to action. "To me it is an absurdity," he wrote, "that the law, which expresses the common will and detests and punishes homicide should itself commit one and, in order to keep citizens from committing murder, order a public one committed." Beccaria believed that the threat of life imprisonment presented the only genuine deterrent to crime. He viewed executions simply as public spectacles which could never inspire the fear they were expected to instill in citizens.

Influenced by Beccaria and the writings of other European visionaries, Dr. Benjamin Rush, a Quaker physician, reformer, and signer of the Declaration of Independence, prepared a paper which he read to intellectuals of the day at the home of Benjamin Franklin. He condemned capital punishment as an offense to reason and humanity. Like Beccaria, he called it degrading and ineffectual and insisted that it was encouraging rather than discouraging crime. "Murder is propagated by hanging for murder," was the sentiment he passed on to his eager listeners. He also called for changes in the prison system and the establishment of a "House of Reform" where capital offenders might be restrained from further harming the innocent—and where they might recover from their antisocial attitudes. He spoke of the remarkable examples set by Grand Duke Leopold II of Tuscany and Catherine of Russia, who had both abolished the death penalty in their domains. Rush is regarded as the father of penal reform in this country and his Philadelphia Society for Alleviating the Miseries of Public Prisons began work which continued into this century under the altered name of the Pennsylvania Prison Society. The Walnut Street Jail, opened in Philadelphia in 1790, marked the beginning of the penitentiary system in the United States.

The call to action was immediately taken up by William Bradford, the attorney general of the state of Pennsylvania who later became the United States attorney general. Bradford was also prepared to defend the view that capital punishment did not work as a deterrent to crime. In his important pamphlet he noted that in the state of Virginia horse stealing was a capital crime. It was also the most commonly committed offense in the state. Furthermore, because it called for execution, it was almost impossible to actually convict a man of horse theft in Virginia! Bradford did want to retain one capital offense, however, and that was murder. He influenced the Pennsylvania legislature to legalize the distinction between first- and second-degree murder, with the death sentence only applicable to the former. This ruling, which was rapidly adopted by other states, defined as second-degree murder any homicide in which there was no evidence of malice or intent. The number of convictions for killing dropped off radically in all jurisdictions which adopted the new distinction. The increasing adequacy of the prison system made this alternative feasible.

The antigallows movement in the United States spread and attracted the support of many well-known social reformers and men of letters. Henry Wadsworth Longfellow took up the cause and by the 1840's Horace Greeley was promoting abolition in his *New York Tribune*. The literature of the movement was idealistic and compassionate. Its leaders

49

were inspired by a general mood of optimism about social betterment and by the writings of such European novelists as Victor Hugo and Charles Dickens, who movingly described the plight of criminals and outcasts. Hugo's Jean Valjean in *Les Miserables* became a highly respected citizen. *The Last Days of a Condemned Man*, also by Victor Hugo, brought sobs to the throats of strong men with its evocation of the mental anguish of a man condemned to death who cries out in despair as he leaves his family forever. The American poet John Greenleaf Whittier put the same theme into verse in "The Gallows and the Human Sacrifice." Criminals were portrayed for the first time as human beings rather than totally depraved monsters.

Liberal thinkers abroad were also pressing for reform. In England the movement progressed at the slowest possible pace pushed by a few dedicated men. Sir Samuel Romilly died a discouraged suicide after his modest bill to abolish the death penalty for thefts from a shop of goods valued at five shillings had been defeated three times. By this time the states of Kentucky and Pennsylvania retained capital punishment for a single offense—first-degree murder. The English judge who ruled on the case reminded Romilly that the law had been written "in the best period of our history" (the age of Cromwell) and he saw "no reason for hazarding an experiment." The proposal was eventually defeated six times and passed in 1832. One of Romilly's triumphs was the repeal of the death penalty for the crime of pickpocketing, which had become capital in 1565. It was not, however, until his second try that he was able to eliminate disemboweling from the punishment for high treason. In the 1830's, when virtually all crimes against property were being punished by imprisonment in the United States and a number of European countries, a nine-year-old boy was hanged in

England for setting fire to a house. A brother and sister, aged seven and eleven, had been hanged together a decade earlier. Another nine-year-old received the death sentence for stealing a few pennies' worth of printer's colors two years later but public opposition caused the penalty to be rescinded. Prisoners being tried on a capital charge did not have right to counsel until 1836 and even a child was expected to conduct his own defense.

But the turning point had come. The first resolution asking for abolition was rejected by Parliament in 1840. By 1860 only five crimes would remain capital in all of England: high treason, murder, piracy with violence, destruction of public arsenals and dockyards, and setting fire to a ship in the port of London.

Around the world the more repellent means of execution had disappeared. The last legal drowning took place in France in 1793. All methods of torture were outlawed when the French adopted the guillotine in 1798. The last burning alive had taken place in 1789—the victim, a counterfeiter. Breaking on the wheel last occurred in Vienna—in 1789. The British gave up disemboweling in 1818 and pressing in 1828.

During the 1820's an American reformer named Edward Livingston drew up a model criminal code for the state of Louisiana. He rebutted all the usual arguments in favor of capital punishment and pointed out the savage criminal code of England—and the alarmingly high incidence of crime—as evidence that harsh laws of capital punishment *encouraged* criminality. Louisiana was not ready for his legal code, but it inspired enlightened changes elsewhere for decades. The legislatures of Maine, Ohio, Massachusetts, New Jersey, New York, and Pennsylvania were constantly studying petitions submitted by abolitionist constituents and forming committees to make recommendations. The "Maine Law" of 1837, which was directly inspired by Livingston's writings, sent capital offenders to the state prison for one year after which a warrant issued by the governor was necessary to bring about execution.

Abolitionist literature stressed the corrupting effect of public hangings on the jeering, cheering, bloodthirsty crowds. In 1834, Pennsylvania became the first state to stop the show and move hangings into the prison yard. New York followed a year later. The governor of Massachusetts, in his annual address, noted that the outstanding characteristic of the decade was "an increasing tenderness for human life." In the spirit of the time he asked that capital punishment in his state be restricted only to murder, but he was unsuccessful. The considerable influence of conservative clergymen helped defeat proposals for reform time after time by condemning the abolitionists as a horde of Unitarians and "Harvard intellectuals." Of course, there was considerable truth in the charge—and there was also a distinct anti-intellectual bias in the religiously orthodox majority of Massachusetts voters.

The governor of New Hampshire called for abolition in 1844 and the matter was decided—against him—in a referendum. But organized societies were springing up and the movement gained further prestige in 1845 when, at a national meeting of state societies, George M. Dallas, the Vice-President of the United States, was elected president of The American Society for the Abolition of Capital Punishment.

And then in 1846, the state of Michigan, which had had no executions since 1830, became the first English-speaking jurisdiction in the world to abolish capital punishment for first-degree murder, the only charge on their books. Rhode Island followed in 1852 and Wisconsin in 1853. In Boston they were still crying out against reform. When one eloquent plea referred to the example set by Catherine of Russia in abolishing the death penalty in the eighteenth century, the clergy denounced the empress as an adulteress and pronounced capital punishment "a moral necessity," which the wicked Russian monarch could not have been expected to comprehend. There was still considerable opposition to change, but most states, except in the south, now retained only two or three capital charges.

Phrenology entered the debate on abolition when noted authorities accompanied petitions with charts which sought to demonstrate that criminals suffered from disease—evidenced by the size and shape of the bumps on their heads—and that they were aroused to further destruction by the existence of capital punishment because their morbid zest for *self*-destruction was titillated by the threat of execution.

During the 1850's and 60's the fire went out of the movement. Reformers became engaged in the better organized and more urgent antislavery movements. Perhaps some early domino theory indicated that state laws would inexorably topple one by one. The horrors of the Civil War may have actually blunted people's sensitivity to the subject of death. Mandatory capital punishment had been virtually eliminated from the statutes of every state in the country and the battle seemed half won. Maine abolished the death penalty, and the federal government, after debates in Congress, reduced its list of dozens of capital crimes to three: murder, treason, and rape, without mandatory death penalty. Around the world great changes had taken place. Public executions had been abolished in England and France. The death penalty was a thing of the past in Denmark, Finland, the Netherlands, Belgium, Switzerland, and Portugal by the 1870's.

An interest in finding a more up-to-date and painless

method of execution led the New York state legislature in the 1880's to approve the dismantling of the gallows in Auburn Prison and the substitution of a scientific new device which had been dubbed "The Electric Chair."

The invention had a curious history. It was the period of rapid electrification in this country and there was fierce competition between companies promoting alternating current and those favoring direct current. A "DC" company staged a dramatic exhibition which was designed to demonstrate the dangers of "AC" to the public. First a cat was led to the current—and promptly electrocuted. Next a dog was sacrificed and finally, we are told, a horse! What effect this had in combatting the competition is not known, but the message got across to those interested in capital punishment that electric current could kill a human being. It also seemed that such a death would be painless and instantaneous.

There had been a number of inexpert hangings in New York in which people had been strangled to death. Execution by electricity seemed humane, clean, and tidy, but it presented a peculiar problem. Cats were one thing—but no one knew quite how much shock was required to kill a man. There were obvious difficulties in staging a trial run. An ape was sacrificed in the chair and the experiment deemed a success.

The electric chair is constructed of wood and is equipped with straps or clamps for the arms, legs, lap, and chest. Wires which come through pipes under the floor carry the current, which is produced by a special generator at the prison. One wire attaches to a head electrode, and is in the form of a helmet with a chin strap. The other is fitted to the leg electrode, which is attached to the prisoner's calf. Both electrodes are faced with sponge which is soaked in salt water to assure a good contact and to minimize burning of the flesh. Current voltage, varied by regulators, can reach 2,200. When this massive current hits it raises the body temperature to 138 degrees, causing immediate reddening of the skin. Death, which occurs within minutes, is due to paralysis of the respiratory and heart muscles. It is hoped that unconsciousness occurs instantaneously although no one is certain of this.

In 1893 a convicted axe murderer named William Kemmler achieved the unenviable distinction of becoming the first man in history to die in the electric chair. His execution followed a long delay during which lawyers unsuccessfully attempted to prevent the procedure on the grounds that killing by electricity was "cruel and unusual punishment." The case was lost in the Supreme Court. On the day of execution Kemmler appeared to be infinitely calmer than the executioner, the official witnesses, or the doctor. An autopsy room had been set up adjoining the death chamber so that medical men might immediately examine the dead body and determine the effects of electrocution. The late Robert Elliott, who was to become the electrocutioner of 387 men and women, tells part of the story in his book *Agent of Death*. The warden escorted Kemmler, who was formally attired in a business suit, into the execution chamber. He introduced the prisoner to the witnesses. "Gentlemen, this is William Kemmler," he said, and Kemmler acknowledged the introduction with a pleasant nod and addressed the audience: "The newspapers have been saying a lot of things about me which were not so," he said. "I wish you all good luck in this world. I believe I am going to a good place." He then removed his jacket and placed it neatly on another chair in the chamber. His vest and shirt were slit in the back to permit the attachment of an electrode (in later years this has been attached to the leg instead). He was strapped to the chair and the headpiece was lowered with *its* electrode. The signal was given to the nervous executioner. One thousand volts were passed through Kemmler's body (two thousand became standard later). Witnesses reported that when the switch was pressed and held, the chair and the man strapped to it began to rock in grotesque fashion due to the effect of the current and the fact that the chair was not bolted to the floor. To the alarmed newsmen and officials it looked as if Kemmler was fighting to get free, although most authorities feel that he lost consciousness immediately. Witnesses shouted to the man at the switch to cut off the current, and it was done. As the horrified audience watched, Kemmler's chest heaved and a thick purple foam came from his mouth. At this sign of life the warden, the doctors, the witnesses, and the electrocutioner all seemed to go to pieces. There were cries of "Turn it on!" and the man at the switch discharged numerous short bursts of current into the body. When he stopped the doctors listened for a heartbeat, found none, and hustled the body off to the autopsy room. A number of newspapers described the ghastly scene and called for a return to hanging. Some indicated to readers that Kemmler actually died when the doctors removed his heart. A thoughtful *New York Times* editorial stated that, although the first use of the chair had been unfortunate, the new machine was obviously a scientific advance and here to stay. Opposition died out, the technique was improved, and by 1906 one hundred condemned prisoners had been electrocuted. The invention caught on in China and the Philippine Islands but was never adopted in Europe, where traditional methods of execution were retained.

America's second innovation was the gas chamber, which

was first used in 1924 in Carson City, Nevada. Reformers in Nevada were anxious to change their image from that of a wild West shooting-and-hanging state to that of a civilized leader in humane up-to-date law enforcement. The bill proposed to the legislature suggested that prisoners condemned to death should be killed by poison gas which would be blown into their cells. This was to be accomplished with no prior notice while the prisoner was asleep. The idea was

57

that the agony of awaiting a preestablished death date would be eliminated, along with the grim walk to the gallows and the macabre but necessary preparations for execution. The prisoner would simply pass his days on death row as peacefully as possible and one morning he would not awaken. The bill was actually signed by the governor and became law, but when it came time to execute a murderer the difficulties of the proposal became clear. There was just no way to fill a prison cell with lethal gas without killing off half the population of the jail. An airtight chamber was constructed with a window to enable the required official witnesses to view the execution without actually participating. The first prisoner to die in the gas chamber, a man named Gee Jon, was led in with a stethoscope attached to his chest. Cyanide pellets tied in a gauze sack hung on a hook under the chair, to which he was strapped. When the room was cleared of everyone but the prisoner and the door closed and sealed, a lever permitted sulfuric acid mixed with water to run into a shallow pan under the chair. Another lever released the cyanide "eggs" and within ten seconds they had dissolved in the acid, the deadly fumes had risen, and soon afterward the prisoner's heartbeat had stopped. An exultant Carson City reporter wrote that Nevada was now "one step further from the savage state."

Fifteen years later in the Nazi death chambers a similar technique allowed poison gas to permeate large tiled rooms through ducts. The system was so efficient that thousands of people, who had been stripped and led into these chambers thinking they were to be given showers, were sealed in, suffocated by fumes within minutes, and carted off to burial pits as soon as the room was ventilated and hosed down.

After Nevada's initiation, eleven states adopted the gas-chamber method of execution. Only seven retained hanging and twenty-four eventually opted for the electric chair. The federal government traditionally uses whatever facilities are standard in the state in which the particular conviction has been upheld.

Shooting has traditionally been reserved for military executions with one exception. The state of Utah offers its condemned prisoners a choice of being shot or hanged. The majority of the condemned over the years have chosen to be shot, and it is of particular interest that in all instances precautions are taken to relieve executioners of remorse in both procedures. If a man is hanged three strings are released simultaneously, one by each of three men assigned to this job. Only one of these actually works the mechanism that opens the drop. The procedure for shooting a condemned man is similar. Five marksmen are appointed and taken to the prison in a car with window shades drawn. Four of the rifles are provided with one round of ammunition each. The prisoner is tied in a chair and a heart-shaped target is pinned over his heart. At the signal all five men discharge their rifles. No one knows which of the five has shot a blank; the other four usually hit the target. Each man can assure himself that he was not the executioner. Traditions such as these, as well as the insistence that a condemned man have a grand "last meal," the consolations of clergy, and the handshake of the warden, are often cited as evidence of the intense feelings of guilt about executions which permeate the public conscience.

During the course of the twentieth century, as state legislatures debated whether or not to outfit their prisons with electric chairs or gas chambers, the move for total abolition continued along with enlightened action and proposals for prison reform. A number of sensational capital cases revitalized the determination of reformers. When famed trial lawyer Clarence Darrow, a leading opponent of capital punishment, saved Leopold and Loeb from execution in the 1920's (*see* Chapter VI), the League for the Abolition of Capital Punishment was formed and attracted many well-known public figures to the cause. In the controversy surrounding three other widely debated cases, the executions of Sacco and Vanzetti in 1927 (*see* Chapter V), of Julius and Ethel Rosenberg in 1953 (*see* Chapter VII), and of Caryl Chessman in 1960 (*see* Chapter VIII), people across the globe cried out that injustice had been done and renewed active agitation for an end to capital punishment.

Others still pursued the notion of finding quieter, comfier, and less mutilating methods of execution and a number of suggestions have been proposed in the past few decades. There has been little debate or attention given to plans for Socrates-like self-administered poisons, lethal injections to be given by doctors, schemes which would force prisoners to subject themselves to fatal medical experiments.

Doctors have refused to consider the idea of violating the Hippocratic oath by administering death-dealing poisons, and giving people fatal diseases—even for the sake of science—could easily become inhuman torture. Another reason such suggestions have failed is that people opposed to the death penalty refuse to even consider the notion of "better" or "worse" means of inflicting the punishment, which they regard as abhorrent in any form. Those in favor feel that our traditional methods are perfectly satisfactory.

The last public execution in this country did not take place until 1936. In that year a black man was hanged in Kentucky while twenty thousand people shoved and jostled to get a better view of the show and newsmen snapped photos. Although Pennsylvania had led the way a century earlier, the taste for watching a good hanging persisted and the legislation that might prevent public participation in this archaic spectacle lagged.

Since that date executions have taken place within the prison and have been attended by somewhere in the vicinity of "twelve reputable citizens," although at the deaths of such famous convicts as the Rosenbergs and Chessman there were dozens. Totally private executions have never been the reformer's aim. The idea of taking a man off alone to be killed unobserved has always struck Americans as smacking of secret police proceedings. Official witnesses represent the public supervising officialdom. They always include some journalists, although the number permitted has been radically reduced over the years and limitations have been placed on reporting lurid details of the death scene. People attending executions must be approved by the prison warden and witnesses are strictly instructed on points of etiquette. At the highly publicized execution of a female murderer several decades ago a reporter concealed a camera in his clothing and caught a picture for his newspaper of the victim as the switch was thrown. Great precautions have been taken ever since to see that this kind of thing is never repeated.

As the twentieth century progressed more states abolished execution. Hawaii and Alaska dropped capital punishment before achieving statehood. Frequently abolition followed a case in which there were strong feelings that an innocent man had been sent to his death. Just as often death penalties were reinstituted after some years of abolition during which one or more particularly brutal crimes had taken place. States which abolished and later restored the death penalty are: Colorado, Washington, South Dakota, Arizona, Missouri, Delaware, and Kansas. When Kansas joined this list in 1944 the warden of the state penitentiary was so strongly opposed that he refused to enforce the punishment and resigned his position.

The actual numbers of executions steadily decreased between 1930 and 1965. From 1930–39 an average of 167 persons per year were executed. In the next decade it was down to 128. Between 1950 and 1959 it dropped to 71. The year 1962 saw 47 persons executed; in 1963, 21; in 1965 there were 7; in 1966 there was 1, and 1967 saw the last 2.

During that period there were fifty thousand first-degree murders in the country and the great majority of the murderers did not receive the death penalty. Of the total number of 3,856 executions which took place during this thoroughly documented thirty-five-year period, 3,332 were for murder, 455 for rape, 24 for armed robbery, 20 for kidnapping, 11 for burglary, 8 for espionage, and 6 for aggravated assault. An additional 33 people were executed under the federal law: 16 for murder, 2 for rape, 1 for armed robbery, 6 for kidnapping, 8 for espionage. The Army and Air Force executed 160 men: 1 deserter, 53 rapists, and 106 murderers. The Navy has not carried out a single execution since 1849. The states varied in numbers of executions from one in thirty-five years in New Hampshire and South Dakota to 366 in Georgia.

In many states old laws remain on the books which have virtually never been invoked. In Georgia castration is a capital offense; in Arkansas colliding with someone while commanding a steamboat is capital; in Tennessee the death penalty can be imposed for assaulting a person with a deadly weapon while wearing a disguise; in South Carolina it is a capital offense to accidentally kill someone while attempting suicide. It is also a capital offense to incite someone else to commit suicide in the state. Other offenses which still legally call for the death penalty include killing someone in a duel, shooting at a train, causing a customer's death by selling him wood alcohol as a beverage, causing death by train wrecking. A few years ago Illinois officially dropped the death penalty for dynamiting.

Despite the pronounced decrease in numbers of executions and the general trend toward eliminating capital offenses from the lists, a number of *extensions* of capital punishment occurred in the twentieth century. In 1902, inspired by the assassination of President McKinley, a federal statute was enacted which made it a capital crime to make an attempt on the life of a high federal official, whether the attempt was successful or not. In 1939 and 1941 two states made assault by a life prisoner (usually on a prison guard) punishable by death. A federal statute was enacted in 1946 which held that providing narcotics to a minor was a capital offense and the same year also saw a new federal statute on espionage violations of the Atomic Energy Act. In 1960 airplane piracy became a specific capital offense, although piracy of one sort or another has been on the roster for centuries in a number of countries.

A widely adopted extension of capital punishment followed one of the most notorious crimes of the century when the Lindbergh Act made it a federal offense to transport a kidnapped man, woman, or child across state lines and provided the death penalty for violations. Laws making kidnapping a capital crime were already in existence in a number of states, but it was felt that local enforcement was not enough when a rash of kidnappings for ransom took place in the 1920's and 30's. The new law allowed the Federal Bureau of Investigation to go into action as soon as kidnappers passed over state lines, and it permitted an *assumption* that this had happened after seven days had passed. In 1956 the interval was reduced to twenty-four hours.

63

At the time of the Lindbergh case, Charles Lindbergh, the boyishly handsome aviator who, five years before had accomplished the first nonstop transatlantic flight, was employed as a technical advisor to two airlines. His wife was the beautiful, poetically gifted young daughter of multimillionaire Dwight Morrow, former ambassador to Mexico and senator from New Jersey. Their first child, Charles Augustus Lindbergh, Jr., was a beguiling twenty-month-old baby. The glamor and adulation which surrounded this enormously attractive and wealthy family was without parallel at the time. It was not until the advent of the John F. Kennedy family that such a phenomenon recurred in this country. The American public was enraptured with the Lindbergh marriage, the birth of their first child, and every publicized detail on their life-style.

One night in March of 1932, the Lindbergh baby, who had been put to bed a few hours earlier by his mother and nurse, was kidnapped from his crib. The entire nation was stunned, horrified, fascinated with the complexities of the ensuing hunt. When Mrs. Lindbergh, who was pregnant with her second child, inserted a precise account of the baby's diet in the newspapers—imploring the kidnapper to adhere to it—young mothers around the country adjusted their own infant-feeding routines to conform. When they read that the child had been ailing with a slight cold and that the kidnapper had left the crib blanket behind on that dark, chill night they heaped covers on their own children and put new locks on nursery windows. A ransom note demanding fifty thousand dollars had been left in young Charles's bedroom. The ransom was paid but the child was never returned. Months later his body was found in a woods—the skull fractured by a heavy instrument. In 1936 a man named Bruno Hauptmann was executed for the crime.

The horrified public demand that such atrocious crimes be halted in the future resulted in the federal Lindbergh Act. Many state legislatures also passed new laws and others increased existing penalties for kidnapping. In all, thirty-five jurisdictions made kidnapping for ransom a capital crime and one (Louisiana) made the death sentence mandatory. This placed kidnapping second after murder in the number of jurisdictions in which the particular crime is a capital offense. Treason, which is third, is capital in twenty states and rape, number four, is capital in eighteen.

By the time of the Supreme Court decision of 1972 Alaska, Hawaii, Iowa, Maine, Michigan, Minnesota, Oregon, West Virginia, and Wisconsin had abolished the death penalty entirely. New Jersey and California had dropped existing death penalty laws within the last few months. New Mexico, New York, North Dakota, Rhode Island, and Vermont had virtually accomplished total abolition. Not one of these states had a prisoner under sentence of death at the time. Idaho, Montana, Nebraska, New Hampshire, South Dakota, and Wyoming had actually carried out only twenty-two executions among them in the decades since 1930. There was no jursidiction in the United States in which juries were not empowered to sentence a man to prison or a mental hospital rather than to death if that seemed more appropriate.

There is an obvious relationship between the decreasing number of executions over the years and the waning of public outcry—except when aroused by some particularly flamboyant or significant case. Executions became so few that they were easy to ignore in an age of great social change and fresher, trendier issues. Everyone knows that we try not to execute the insane—although experts feel that the majority of murderers are mentally disturbed. When the crime is sufficiently horrifying—as in the assassination of a President—the issue does not arise at all. John Wilkes Booth was shot in a barn while attempting to elude capture and Lee Harvey Oswald was informally executed by Jack Ruby, but Leon Czolgosz, who shot McKinley, and Charles Guiteau, who killed Garfield, were hastily tried and hanged. Both were thought to be mad.

We oppose executing minors, although unused and primitive state laws still list the minimum age for execution at anywhere from seven to eighteen. Over seventy teen-agers have been executed in the past fifty years, including a fourteen-year-old black boy electrocuted in South Carolina for murder in 1944. Newspaper readers felt reassured when a Gallup Poll of the 1950's elicited the satisfying information that most people preferred the idea of being electrocuted to that of being shot, gassed, or hanged. Electrocution, after all, was firmly established as our most common means of execution.

Recent public opinion polls show that approximately half the American people are opposed to the death penalty at this time and that the number of those in favor has decreased radically since the first poll, taken in 1936. Americans pro and con told pollsters that they disapprove of executing people under twenty-one years of age and the majority in favor of capital punishment felt, when asked, that women convicted of murder should be executed as well as men. More men than women favor the death penalty as do greater numbers of residents of the far-western states compared with those from the East, South, and Midwest. Asked on a Gallup Poll to give their reasons for favoring or disapproving the death sentence most answered by citing Scripture. Those who wished to retain the penalty felt that it was justified by the Bible; those who would see it abolished found it "against the teaching of our Lord." The second most common response in favor of the death penalty was that it served as a deterrent to further murders.

We have no comparative statistics from the nations which have abandoned capital punishment in this century and can only guess at the actual effect of majority opinion on abolition. During World War II a number of abolitionist countries enacted temporary laws to permit the execution of traitors, collaborators with enemy countries, or men and women found guilty of war crimes. The death penalty was outlawed in the Russia of Catherine the Great and later reinstituted in the Soviet Union, but only for political crimes. Murderers were exiled to Siberia along with a great variety of other offenders. Capital punishment has now been extended to such economic crimes as counterfeiting and money speculation and also to murder, spying, and sabotage.

The following countries have either abolished the death penalty or retained it only for exceptional wartime or martial law offenses: Argentina, Australia (Queensland, Federal Territory, New South Wales, Tasmania), Austria, Belgium, Bolivia, Brazil, Canada, Colombia, Costa Rica, Denmark, Dominican Republic, Ecuador, Finland, West Germany, Honduras, Iceland, India, Israel, Italy, Liechtenstein, Luxembourg, Mexico (twenty-nine of thirty-two states), Monaco, Nepal, Netherlands (also Netherlands Antilles and Surinam), New Zealand, Nicaragua, Norway, Panama, Portugal, San Marino, Sweden, Switzerland, United Kingdom, Uruguay, Vatican City State, Venezuela. In addition there are abolitionist states and territories in both hemispheres. Some have abolished the death penalty *de jure*—by specific legislative or constitutional provision. Others, such as Belgium, Liechtenstein, Luxembourg, and

Vatican City State, have abolished it *de facto*—by established custom.

The death penalty has been retained in most African, Asian, and Iron Curtain countries as well as in France and Spain. Around the globe, in hundreds of tongues, the same arguments for and against capital punishment have been debated by lay citizens, jurists, and legislators. There is no question about the fact that those opposed are winning the battle to bring about an end to the law of retaliatory vengeance in the twentieth century.

Four cases which occurred in this country in the past fifty years are vividly recalled whenever capital punishment is under discussion. They have been cited in abolitionist proposals in America and in many foreign lands. Each of the trials was accompanied by international publicity; each reactivated the fight for total abolition of the death penalty. In these notorious dramas seven defendants—six men and one woman—struggled to escape execution. Five lost the battle and were put to death by legal authority.

The two who were permitted to live—Nathan Leopold and Richard Loeb—had confessed to a cold-blooded and brutal crime. Those who died, died unconfessed, in an aura of intense controversy. Nicola Sacco and Bartolomeo Vanzetti have been judged innocent by posterity. Julius and Ethel Rosenberg died for their alleged role in a conspiracy. The other conspirators served from ten to eighteen years in prison. Caryl Chessman was executed for a commonplace sexual offense on a technical charge of kidnapping after his case became a political football.

The following four chapters deal with these six men and one woman whose trials, sentences, and fates serve as demonstration of the cruel, unusual, and discriminatory manner in which the ultimate penalty has been sought and enforced in our time.

# SACCO AND VANZETTI

AT MIDAFTERNOON on April 15, 1920, a robbery and murder took place in the small city of South Braintree, Massachusetts. What began as a rather ordinary brutality developed into one of the most famous criminal trials and convictions of all times. Belief in the guilt or innocence of the accused men, Nicola Sacco and Bartolomeo Vanzetti, separated society into opposing camps. The leading newspapers declared themselves firmly "pro" or eloquently "anti" the court's decision. Controversy about the conduct of the trial and the personalities and politics involved brought impassioned criticism of American justice from around the world.

As far as Sacco and Vanzetti themselves were concerned, the tragic events which began that spring afternoon came to an end when the two men were put to death in the electric chair seven years later. But reexamination of the circumstances of the crime and reinterpretation of the trial testimony of over 150 witnesses, which fills six heavy volumes, has continued until the present.

Had Sacco and Vanzetti been spared the death sentence the crime of which they were accused would have been ignored by the world. Instead, they achieved the unenviable status of martyrdom. Their execution rekindled the fight against capital punishment which had flagged amidst the more immediate problems of the World War I and postwar periods. State and national leagues dedicated to the abolition of capital punishment sprang into being and attracted the support of thousands. Famed attorney Clarence Darrow became the most prominent foe of the death penalty and the most eloquent speaker for the cause. Around the world, in private discussions and in the halls of legislatures where new criminal laws were under debate the case became a touchstone. It remains so today. Whenever the possibility of judicial error is used as argument against the irrevocable sentence of death the case of the two Italian immigrants is brought forth in evidence.

In 1969 the only surviving attorney who had been directly involved in the proceedings, Herbert B. Ehrmann, wrote his second book about the case. He titled it, with particular aptness, *The Case That Will Not Die.* In the half century since the event, artists, poets, dramatists, novelists, film makers, and television producers have told and retold the story of two simple workingmen whose names became known around the world.

South Braintree, which is situated ten miles south of Boston, was, in 1920, a town of about ten thousand people. There was no national bank and the payroll money for the city's two shoe factories was customarily sent down by train from the National Shawmut Bank in Boston. The train was met by the American Express agent, who took the iron cashbox to the two factories, Slater and Morrill and Walker and Kneeland. Frederick Parmenter was the paymaster at

Slater and Morrill and, after a clerk had divided the company's sixteen-thousand-dollar payroll into numerous small envelopes placed in two large boxes, he and his assistant, Alessandro Berardelli, picked up the boxes for delivery to the plant which was located a few blocks from the factory office. It was 3 P.M. as they walked down the main street of South Braintree. Suddenly two men armed with pistols darted onto the sidewalk firing at the paymaster and guard. The wounded men fell to the ground as pedestrians scattered. A car containing two other men, with a third crouched on the running board waving a revolver, pulled up to the scene. The gunmen grabbed the cashboxes, and leapt into the car, which took off in the direction of the railroad tracks. A rifle could be seen pointing backward through a missing rear window and as the car retreated one of the occupants tossed out a shower of tacks to puncture the tires of would-be pursuers.

Berardelli died on the pavement a few moments later, as horrified men and women rushed to his assistance. Parmenter was taken to the hospital where surgery was performed, but he died the next day. The car, a new seven-passenger Buick touring model, was found by mounted hunters. It had been abandoned in the woods eight miles from the scene of the crime. Nearby distinct tracks of another smaller car were noted. Police surmised that the bandits had left the conspicuous murder car and escaped in a second car which met them at this prearranged site. Some townspeople later recalled having seen both the touring car and a small dusty sedan near the scene earlier in the day. The Buick was found to have been stolen the previous November from a reputable citizen of nearby Needham.

Three weeks later Sacco and Vanzetti were arrested as suspects in the crime by the South Braintree police. Both were immigrants who had come to this country in 1908. Although they had been in the United States for twelve years they had associated almost exclusively with other members of the Italian community. Neither was a citizen; both spoke very limited English. Sacco, twenty-nine at the time, was a married man with a young son and a pregnant, pretty red-haired wife named Rosina. He was a skilled edge-cutter in a shoe factory in nearby South Stoughton and he also sometimes worked as night watchman at the plant. Vanzetti, who was thirty-two, was a single man who boarded with an Italian family in Plymouth. He had practiced a number of trades—pastry cook, kitchen helper, railroad laborer, bricklayer's helper—and had lived in several American cities. Currently, he was working as a fish peddler in Plymouth. Both men were anarchists, who had met and become friends through their shared sympathies and political activities in the community.

They were arrested after the South Braintree police chief received a telephone call he had been awaiting from the owner of a garage. It notified him that a group of men had come to pick up a dilapidated 1912 Overland sedan which had been left for repairs. Through a chain of investigations the police chief had come to believe that this was the car which had made the tracks found near the abandoned Buick. When the owner and three other Italians arrived to claim the car, the garage proprietor refused to let them take it because they did not have 1920 license plates. Two men left on a motorcycle with sidecar. The remaining two, Sacco and Vanzetti, boarded a streetcar to return home. They were arrested while riding on the streetcar and taken into custody.

The police informed their captives that they were being held as "suspicious characters"—and they must have been intensely gratified to discover how very suspicious the two men seemed. They denied knowing the friends from whom they had just parted at the garage. They were nervous and evasive when answering questions about their political beliefs, their movements that evening, and their reasons for wanting the car. Most striking of all was the fact that both men were armed. Sacco carried a loaded Colt .38 caliber pistol, Vanzetti a fully loaded revolver. To the police it seemed obvious that these gun-toting anarchists were off to commit another robbery.

The lies Sacco and Vanzetti told the police at the time of their arrest were, however, based on entirely different fears. The men were not told until the next day that they were being held as suspects in the South Braintree robbery and murder. It was their immediate impression—and the idea was extremely alarming—that they had been seized because of their political affiliations. As was brought out later in their court testimony, they had gone with Boda and Orciani to pick up Boda's car, which they intended to use to rid their homes of large supplies of anarchist literature. Recent events had increased their fears of raids, arrest, and perhaps even deportation.

Half a century separates us from the period under discussion and it is not easy to recreate the political climate of the day. The postwar period was a time of industrial strikes and violence. Communism, which originated with Karl Marx's *Communist Manifesto* in 1848, had become a political reality in Russia with the Bolshevik Revolution of 1917. In this country aliens and radicals of many loyalties and persuasions were grouped together and fearfully dubbed "The Red Menace." The First Communist International, organized in the midnineteenth century, was an attempt to cut across national boundaries and embrace the aspirations of

73

poor workers in all capitalist societies. The threat was not felt here until the Russian Revolution established a solid national base for future international activity. Lenin, the first Communist leader in Russia, founded the Third Communist International, with the announced purpose of repeating the Russian experience in other industrial countries.

At first there had been hope in the West that the Communist triumph could be undone and to this end United States and British troops fought alongside Russian counter-revolutionary troops until the end of 1919. By then the facts could no longer be ignored, and the United States reacted with hysteria. The American Communist party was founded and Attorney General Alexander Palmer countered with a witch hunt—"a dragnet for Reds all over the country."

On the second anniversary of the Russian Revolution, government agents backed up by local police forces broke into headquarters of the Communist party. Without warrants they rounded up citizens and noncitizens, broke into files and safes, wrecked property. Under the provisions of the 1918 Deportation Act hundreds of anarchist and Communist aliens, suspected of sympathy with the Soviet Russian regime and involvement in a conspiracy to overthrow the United States government, were deported. Bombs, thought to be the work of anarchists, were mailed to prominent Americans. One, which was being hand delivered to the home of Attorney General Palmer, went off prematurely, damaging the front of his house and blowing the carrier to bits. Palmer announced a Communist plot to kill off high American officials and force United States diplomatic recognition of Soviet Russia. When the deportation of the leading anarchist figure in the country was followed by explosions in eight cities, the *New York Times* attributed the bombings to Bolsheviks; other newspapers blamed anarchists. Although "anarchists"—who oppose *all* forms of government as oppressive—cannot be automatically identified with "Communists," to the American public the terms were synonymous and both spelled MENACE.

In January of 1920 simultaneous Justice Department raids took place in thirty-three cities and three thousand men and women were held for deportation, although only four hundred were eventually sent back across the Atlantic. In Boston five hundred immigrants were herded through the streets chained. Leading lawyers of the day spoke out against the illegal practices of the Justice Department, but to no avail.

On May 4, 1920, an anarchist leader named Salsedo, who was being held for questioning by agents of the Department of Justice in New York, fell from a fifth-story window to his death. Rumors that he had been pushed swept anarchist circles. It was on the day after Salsedo's death that Sacco and Vanzetti were taken into custody. In Sacco's pocket police found a notice written by Vanzetti in Italian. The message invited people to attend a talk that he would have given about Salsedo and the current scare on the following Sunday.

There had been numerous eyewitnesses to the South Braintree crime and the group was quickly rounded up and brought to the police station where they were first shown an assortment of rogues' gallery photographs which had been sent down from Boston. Quite a few picked out the picture of a man named Anthony Palmisano and positively identified him as one of the bandits. Unfortunately, Palmisano was found to have been sitting cozily in a Buffalo jail since the preceding January.

After this embarrassment, the police were delighted to be able to produce live suspects. Sacco and Vanzetti were brought before the witnesses. The procedure at the identification sessions was highly unusual. In such instances a suspect is invariably grouped with others of the same race and similar age and appearance in a police lineup. The witness is then asked if he can spot in this group the criminal he saw commit the deed. This is a precautionary measure to prevent suggesting to the witnesses that an identification has already been made. Most people are sufficiently suggestible so that false identification is a strong possibility—particularly by witnesses who have been on the scene of a frightening event without the time or peace of mind to study the criminal carefully. Sacco and Vanzetti, however, were exhibited alone. The witnesses were aware that they had already been taken into custody on suspicion of having committed the crime. Furthermore, they were ordered to assume banditlike postures—to pretend they were crouched on the running board or standing with a pistol over a fallen victim. After the pantomime a number of the witnesses thought that these Italians did indeed seem to be two of the foreign-looking men they had seen that afternoon in South Braintree.

The trial took place in a courtroom in Dedham. Judge Webster Thayer—tiny, elderly, and beak-nosed—was a caricaturist's delight. He would be widely criticized for his conduct of the trial along with the district attorney, Frederick Katzmann. Fred Moore, attorney for the defense, was a Western lawyer who had previously defended other radicals in legal actions.

Jury selection took four very long days during which 650 candidates, as opposed to the usual 75 or so, were screened. It was known that the case would be long and the jury would be confined for the entire time, sleeping in the courthouse, restrained from seeing family or outsiders or reading reports of the case in the newspapers. Potential jurors, dismayed at this prospect and fearful of anarchist reprisals if the defendants were found guilty, pretended deafness, announced themselves unalterably opposed to the death penalty, and claimed chronic illnesses. Moore hoped to select jurors who were not opposed to organized labor. Judge Thayer had his own criteria as did Katzmann. Only seven of the required twelve jurors had been selected when the list of 500 veniremen was exhausted. The sheriff went out on the street, rounding up lodge members leaving a Masonic meeting, snatching a bridegroom at his wedding supper and some musicians from a band concert. When the jury had been picked almost all the names were Anglo-Saxon. None were Italian.

The trial lasted seven weeks. Fifty-nine witnesses testified for the Commonwealth of Massachusetts and ninety-nine for the defendants. All witnesses agreed that five men had been involved in the crime and they were invariably described as looking like "foreigners" or "Italians." A number of men and women thought Sacco and Vanzetti were two of the bandits; an equal number felt they could not so identify them. One of the Commonwealth's chief witnesses was a bookkeeper named Mary Splaine who had viewed the scene from a window. She testified that she had seen Sacco from a distance of about sixty feet for an interval of approximately one and one-half to three seconds as he was seated in the retreating car, traveling at about eighteen miles an hour. A year later at the trial she described sixteen exact details of his person including the tinge of his complexion, the height of his forehead, the length in inches of his hair, its styling, and the size and shape of his hand, which she saw resting on the back of the car's front seat. Miss Splaine had been one of the witnesses who positively selected Palmisano from his photograph before seeing Sacco. In a later attempt to gain a new trial an internationally famous psychiatry professor from Harvard was asked by the defense to study her testimony and he deemed it impossible that a witness could so precisely examine a man under such circumstances. She had, of course, given an accurate picture of Sacco, but she had also had every opportunity to study him in court before she took the stand.

Identification of Vanzetti was also flimsy. A railroad employee, who had been ordered by the gunmen to open the gate so that they might drive across the tracks, identified Vanzetti as the driver, although all other witnesses had described the driver as a frail, sickly-looking, blond young man. Vanzetti was tall, dark, and balding with a luxuriant droopy mustache. In all, seven witnesses identified Sacco; four identified Vanzetti. The defense offered twelve witnesses who could swear to the fact that Vanzetti had spent the day peddling fish in Plymouth and that Sacco had been in Boston. Nicola Sacco, an avid worker who rarely missed a day at the shoe plant, had not been at work on April 15, 1920. His mother had died recently in Italy and it was his contention that he had gone on that day to the consular office in Boston to arrange for a visa to return home and visit his father. He said that when he arrived he was turned away because the photograph he brought was not regulation passport size. A consular official called to testify recalled the incident. Sacco further alleged that he had had lunch with a friend and had seen other acquaintances before leaving Boston. All those who testified to the alibis of both men were Italians and Katzmann sharply cross-examined them, pointing up their friendship to the defendants and casting doubt on their reliability in remembering dates. An interpreter was employed by the court and dismissed by order of the defense for faulty translation. He was later sentenced to jail for attempting to bribe a judge.

Another bit of evidence was a cap, said to have been found near the slain men. The prosecution produced the cap and claimed that it belonged to Sacco. He tried it on in court, denying ownership. To a newspaper reporter-cartoonist it seemed much too small and he drew it perched on top of Sacco's head. To the prosecutor it was a perfect fit—a Cinderella-like positive identification.

Ballistics experts testified for both sides and their testimony became highly controversial. The question was whether or not one of the fatal bullets could be proven to have been fired by Sacco's gun, since there was no question that it came from a similar weapon. The highly technical issue was never satisfactorily determined. The final opinion was that the bullet "was consistent with being fired" from Sacco's gun. Vanzetti's revolver was said by the prosecution to have been taken from the dying Berardelli, who was known to possess and sometimes carry a weapon of this type. No one, however, had actually seen the guard with a gun that day nor did any eyewitness testify to having seen either gunman pick up a revolver from the street or sidewalk. Sacco testified that he had acquired his pistol when he worked as a night watchman. Vanzetti, who said that he used his revolver occasionally to shoot in the woods, also claimed that he bought it for self-protection since when he went to purchase fish he often carried considerable cash. But the firearms seemed even more incriminating when the two testified that they were the variety of anarchists who were also pacifists—opposed to any sort of violence whatsoever.

The views of the two men on violence and warfare came out during the most controversial and irregular part of the trial. It must be remembered that the majority of Americans at this time had translated the patriotic fervor left over from the war into suspicion, fear, and hostility toward foreigners, aliens, and radical political groups. Katzmann, in his examination of Sacco and Vanzetti, played on all the prejudices of the jury members by sharply questioning the accused murderers about their political beliefs. He formed, by his questions, a picture of the defendants as ungrateful aliens and unpatriotic draft dodgers—men who benefited from the privileges of living in America without returning loyalty and love. He exploited their "foreignness"—their difficulties with the language, their unconventional view of a self-governed society. Judge Thayer, to the astonishment and horror of interested liberals who attended the trial and jurists and writers who later studied the case, permitted this line of questioning to continue, although there was not the slightest relationship between the accused men's political views and the crime for which they were being tried.

Both Sacco and Vanzetti spoke on the stand of their flight to Mexico to escape being drafted when the United States entered World War I. They said that as pacifists they could not serve in any army. Actually, as noncitizens who had not taken out their first papers they would have been exempt, but this fact escaped them because of their language difficulty. The friends had spent two unhappy months as laborers in Mexico, and then slipped back across the border. Opposition to the war was rare at that time except among such generally unadmired groups as the Industrial Workers of the World and assorted socialists, anarchists, and pacifists.

Judge Thayer followed up on the image of the men as draft dodgers. He scattered his charge to the jury with references to "our soldier boys." He commended the jurymen,

*Bartolomeo Vanzetti (l.) and Nicola Sacco (r.) are shown arriving at the courthouse in Dedham where they were tried for murder.*

saying that they had responded to the call of civic duty "like the true soldier responding to that call in the spirit of supreme American loyalty." The prosecution emphasized the matter of "consciousness of guilt"—the silent evidence of the fact that the men, when arrested, lied to the police about their activities. No motive for the crime was ever demonstrated. Vanzetti had never cared about money; Sacco had a good salary for a workingman and had fifteen hundred dollars in a savings account. No trace of the sixteen thousand dollars was ever found and no large contribution to the anarchist cause could be shown to have been made at that time. No serious attempt was made to find the other three bandits alleged to have been participants in the crime. Boda disappeared from the country; Orciani had punched a time clock at work that day. The trunk of a man named Coacci, with whom Boda had lived, was seized as he reached Italy after deportation. It contained old clothes but not sixteen thousand dollars.

The jury recessed for less than five hours and returned a verdict on July 14, 1921. Both men had been found guilty of murder in the first degree—which meant the death penalty. The defendant Nicola Sacco shouted out, *"Sono innocente!"* His wife Rosina screamed at the jury, "They kill my man!" The assistant district attorney was found in tears by the astonished Moore as the courtroom emptied. "This is the saddest thing that ever happened to me in my life," he said, in what should have been a moment of victory.

During the following six years the case came into international prominence. Many believed the men were innocent, that they had not been given a fair trial, and were to be executed for their political beliefs and not for committing murder. A Sacco-Vanzetti Defense Committee, originally manned entirely by Italian political radicals, attracted

Back Bay Bostonians, reformers, and intellectuals from universities and from the arts. Communist-inspired demonstrations took place in front of American embassies in Paris, Zurich, Basle, and Geneva. Bombs were sent to embassies in Argentina, Brazil, Chile, Mexico, and Panama.

Two days after the decision, the defense attorney filed a motion for a new trial on the grounds that the verdict had contradicted the weight of the evidence presented. Thayer denied the motion. Over the years there would be five more supplementary motions for a new trial, each one postponing the execution of the sentence. One of these was based on the fact that the foreman of the jury had said to a friend who expressed doubt that Sacco and Vanzetti were guilty, "Damn them, they ought to hang them anyway." Affidavits attacking the alteration in the stories of some of the eyewitnesses and ballistics experts were filed and "new and independent testimony" was offered when a man named Ray Gould was located. Gould had come to the factory with a paste for resharpening razor blades which he peddled outside the gates on payday. The bandits had actually fired on him but missed their mark. He had not been called in the trial and was ready to swear that these were the wrong men. The motion for a new trial was denied.

Moore remained convinced that the holdup had been the work of professionals. In 1925 a convict named Celestino Madeiros, in the cell next to Sacco's, handed over a written confession which said that he had taken part in the murder of the paymaster and guard and that Sacco and Vanzetti had not been members of the group at all. Moore—whose brash informal ways had noticeably irritated Thayer at the trial—had been replaced by a lawyer named Thompson. Thompson's assistant, Herbert Ehrmann, thoroughly investigated the Madeiros confession and found evidence that a professional group of criminals from Providence known as the Morelli gang had accomplished the robbery and murder. Photographs of Joseph Morelli show that he bore a remarkable physical resemblance to Nicola Sacco. Thompson argued that this new information was reason to reopen the case. He also argued that Thayer's personal prejudices and hatred for the defendants had distorted his handling of the trial. He had referred to Sacco and Vanzetti outside the courtroom as "those anarchist bastards."

Thayer heard and denied each motion to hold a new trial. Sacco-Vanzetti committees were organized around the world. In this country the American Civil Liberties Union joined in the cause and demonstrations took place at universities. Many Americans expressed the view that even if guilty, Sacco and Vanzetti should not be executed because of the extent of European disapproval. Noted intellectuals spoke out, raised money for the defense, and wrote lengthy letters to the editors of newspapers and magazines.

A number of influential Boston women had interested themselves in the case from the start. They had attended the trial, supported the Defense Committee, and contributed funds. They also dedicated themselves to visiting the condemned men in jail. The convicts were not allowed to work and were wretchedly idle. The Boston women gave them English lessons. Both men greatly increased their ability with the language during the tormenting years of motions, appeals, and delays. Both became prolific letter writers. Vanzetti's first attempt at a letter in English was written to Mrs. Evans, his most devoted teacher:

> Tank to you from the bottom of my earth for your confidence in my innocence; I am so. I did not splittel a drop of blood, or still a cent in all my life . . . I wish to con-

vince my fellow men that only with virtue and honesty is possible for us to find a little happyness in this world.

Sacco, tormented with loneliness, wrote to Mrs. Evans about his wife and two young children and the happy years before his conviction. "Those day they was a some happy day," he concluded. Vanzetti, always the more able and eloquent of the two, wrote poetically of "The blissing green . . . the mistic dawn . . . the glory of the moon" in his father's Italian garden. Vanzetti also wrote articles for an anarchist journal, attempted a short autobiography, and wrote a piece about the trial.

When the Massachusetts Supreme Court refused to review Judge Thayer's decision, Vanzetti wrote to Mrs. Blackwell, another staunch supporter: "Yesterday we got the last struck. It end all. We are doomed beyond any kind of doubts."

In the USSR Stalin spoke of Sacco and Vanzetti at the Party Congress. In Paris dancer Isadora Duncan debated the case publicly with a judge from Chicago. The Paris newspaper *Le Temps* wanted them spared if innocent or guilty. The *London Times* felt it infinitely cruel to keep men in suspense for so long. H. L. Mencken, Walter Lippmann, John Dewey, H. G. Wells, George Bernard Shaw, Edna St. Vincent Millay, and a host of other prominent writers called for pardon. When Felix Frankfurter, then a prominent Harvard Law School professor, wrote in the staid *Atlantic Monthly* attacking the conduct of the trial and the entire Massachusetts judicial system, sympathy for the defendants reached beyond liberal and left-wing political groups and American and European intellectuals. Discussions were held in women's club meetings, in small-town libraries, in schools in the Midwest and far West.

Although pleas were made for his mercy in seventeen thousand letters, the governor of Massachusetts, Alvan T. Fuller, did not feel it appropriate to reopen the case because of the harassment of radicals. Soon, however, he also had in hand petitions produced by the American Civil Liberties Union from more than sixty law faculties. He appointed a committee of three distinguished men to study the case and make recommendations. The men were A. Lawrence Lowell, president of Harvard, Samuel W. Stratton, president of the Massachusetts Institute of Technology, and Robert Grant, a novelist and probate court judge. Fuller visited the condemned men in jail and Vanzetti was cheered. "I like to tell you that he gave me a good heartfull sake hand, as I lef. I may be wrong, but I don't believe that a man like that is going to burn us on a case like ours," he wrote to a friend. The Defense Committee handed the governor a petition signed by half a million people.

Execution had been set for July 10, 1927, and the Defense Committee was desperate. Charles Lindbergh had crossed the Atlantic that May and he was unsuccessfully wired for support while on a triumphal tour of the country. Telegrams reached President Coolidge on vacation at Yellowstone National Park. The Lowell Committee was still hearing witnesses and the execution date was moved to August 10. On August 4 newspapers announced that Governor Fuller, in agreement with the recommendations of the Advisory Committee, had refused clemency. Bombs exploded in subway stations in New York. Sacco wrote his anarchist supporters: "From the death cell, we are just informe from the Defense Committee that the governor Fuller has descide to kill us Ag. the 10th." Heywood Broun wrote in the *New York Evening World*, "It is not every prisoner who has a President of Harvard University throw on the switch for him."

Ten thousand people gathered in Union Square in New York under a banner reading I NEVER SPILLED BLOOD. It was a Vanzetti quote with corrected spelling. In London, ten thousand gathered in Trafalgar Square and marched on the American Embassy on a summer Sunday to find that the only person on the premises was a British caretaker. Five thousand more demonstrated in Paris. On execution day, August 10, Governor Fuller granted a twelve-day respite while the Supreme Judicial Court considered a further motion. The Defense Committee brought Vanzetti's sister from Italy and she was photographed with the distraught Rosina Sacco. Sacco and Vanzetti were on hunger strikes. Roses were sent to Vanzetti's cell on his thirty-ninth birthday. On August 19 the Court refused to agree that Thayer's prejudices had denied the men a fair trial. Headlines roared: "Exceptions Overruled" . . . "Sacco and Vanzetti Must Die in Chair." A number of leading newspapers commended the verdict, while others supported the theory of innocence until the end.

On the last day Vanzetti wrote Dante, the son of Sacco:

> . . . Remember and know also, Dante, that if your father and I would have been cowards and hypocrits and rinnegators of our faith, we would not have been put to death. They would not even have convicted a lebbrous dog; not even executed a deadly poisoned scorpion on such evidence as that they framed against us.

The night of the execution Charlestown Prison was ringed with over a thousand police, riot squad personnel, patrolmen, and state troopers. A death march was held in front of the State House and crowds circled the prison outside the lines. Sacco, while being strapped to the electric chair, cried out in Italian, "Long live anarchy" and then in

English, "Farewell my wife and child and all my friends." Vanzetti addressed the witnesses: "I wish to say to you that I am innocent. I have never done a crime, some sins, but never any crime. I am an innocent man."

The bodies were taken to a Boston funeral parlor where one hundred thousand people came to view the two famous men in their coffins. One woman brought a sign bearing a quotation: "DID YOU SEE WHAT I DID TO THOSE ANARCHIST BASTARDS?"—JUDGE WEBSTER THAYER. Thayer's home was destroyed by a bomb five years later. In 1959 a judiciary committee of the Massachusetts legislature was asked to grant Sacco and Vanzetti a posthumous pardon. They refused to consider the issue.

Literature about the case began to pile up almost immediately. The artist Ben Shahn painted twenty-three scenes of the trial which he called "The Passion of Sacco and Vanzetti." One showed the men in their coffins with the Lowell Committee standing over them holding lilies and Judge Thayer raising a righteous hand in the background. Maxwell Anderson wrote two plays about the case and in the second, *Winterset*, he gives the judge these words:

> . . . It's better,
> As any judge can tell you, in such cases,
> holding the common good to be worth more
> than small injustice, to let the record stand,
> let one man die. For justice, in the main,
> is governed by opinion.

The serious analytical books that have been written since come to various conclusions. Robert Montgomery in *Sacco and Vanzetti: The Murder and the Myth* seeks to demonstrate that the trial was fair and the case blown up to unnatural proportions by the Communists. Others remain convinced of the innocence of both men and the impossibility of anarchists gaining a fair trial in the state of Massachusetts in 1921. Francis Russell, who wrote *Tragedy in Dedham* because he believed the men innocent, concluded his study with the conviction that Vanzetti was innocent but that Sacco may have been implicated. Ehrmann casts blame on the Morelli gang. Many others have written and many questions will never be answered. Virtually everyone concerned with the case has now died and the story of the shoemaker and the fish peddler remains a tragic period piece—a warning to be recalled whenever prejudice threatens the course of just and impartial investigation. A recent film about the case portrays the men as innocent victims of a witch hunt more terrifying than that which hit Salem in the seventeenth century. Darrow wrote that those found guilty of grave crimes should be imprisoned so that the next generation could re-evaluate the case. Would Sacco and Vanzetti have been found guilty of murder and executed a generation later when the climate had changed? Twenty-five years afterward, the Rosenberg case would pose the same question. How many Saccos and Vanzettis have died because the atmosphere of the times determined their fate? How many thousands of men who have incontestably committed crimes as abhorrent as those of which Sacco and Vanzetti were accused escaped the death penalty because their actions occurred in more peaceful times or in a state which had abolished capital punishment or because their trials took place before a more merciful judge? The case of Sacco and Vanzetti is a prime example of what Justice Brennan meant when he wrote that the infliction of the death penalty is "little more than a lottery system."

Perhaps the most famous and prophetic statement on the matter of the Braintree murders was made by Vanzetti himself. This is what he said to a newspaper reporter in the last days of his life:

If it had not been for this thing, I might have lived out my life talking at street corners to scorning men. I might have died, unmarked, unknown, a failure. Now we are not a failure. This is our career and our triumph. Never in our full life can we hope to do such work for tolerance, for justice, for man's understanding of man, as we now do by an accident. Our words—our lives—our pains—nothing! The taking of our lives—lives of a good shoemaker and a poor fish peddler—all! That last moment belongs to us—that agony is our triumph.

# LEOPOLD AND LOEB

THE IDEA of the perfect crime is endlessly tantalizing to mystery writers and mystery readers. Many imaginative children and adults have at one time or another tried to dream up an elaborately clever plan which would totally baffle the most experienced police investigators and the wiliest detectives. In 1924 two teen-agers named Richard Loeb and Nathan Leopold acted out such a fantasy. They plotted the details and then selected a totally innocent person and murdered him—simply for the "thrill."

When Nathan Leopold and Richard Loeb became names known around the world, Nicola Sacco and Bartolomeo Vanzetti had not yet been executed. There were hopes that they might be spared the death penalty and activists were engaged in pressure toward this end. No one rushed to urge that Leopold and Loeb be spared. They seemed certain to hang. The abolitionist cause had many impassioned spokesmen but they were otherwise occupied. Sacco and Vanzetti were regarded as the innocent victims of persecution; Leopold and Loeb were confessed murderers who had "earned" their punishment. Many seemed to have forgotten that, if capital punishment is wrong, it is wrong for the guilty as well as for the innocent.

It was after the sentencing that the full significance of the case became apparent. Although the judge's decision brought forth outraged expressions in support of the death penalty, Darrow's eloquent plea for the lives of the youthful murderers inspired new organizations dedicated to abolition. Public debates and discussions were held which received the critical attention of thousands of thoughtful citizens, leading lawyers, legislators, and judges. Many years later, when the news from Stateville Penitentiary revealed the story of the useful and dedicated life being led by Nathan Leopold, the case gained further and ultimately even greater importance as demonstration of the value of a life lived rather than a life denied.

At the time of their arrest in 1924, however, it was the circumstances of the murder which horrified and fascinated newspaper readers everywhere. The case became known as "The Crime of the Century."

It is difficult to imagine that such a crime would achieve this much notoriety today. Fifty years ago it was unbelievable that educated and wealthy young men with devoted parents and every expectation for rich full lives would ever break the law in *any* respect, much less commit murder. Today we have heard a great deal about middle-class crime, about brutal forms of juvenile delinquency at all social and economic levels, about sadists and masochists and psychopathic personalities. We are more sophisticated about mental illness and we know that the rich can be just as "sick" as the poor. The twenties were the years of the infancy of psychiatry in this country and when the prosecuting attorney in the Leopold-Loeb case asked a testifying psychiatrist if "psychotic" meant "bughouse" he was certainly no more ignorant about the subject than most Americans.

The fact that there had been a bond of homosexual attraction between the two boys was considered so scandalous that testimony about this aspect of their relationship was literally given in whispers. The psychiatrist-witness left the stand, approached the bench, and conveyed his information to the judge in a low voice so that others in the courtroom might not hear. Many years have now passed since Dr. Kinsey first illuminated this misunderstood subject by gathering statistics on the considerable percentage of men and women in this country who are homosexual or bisexual. Even more revealing were his figures relating to the very large number of people who, although exclusively heterosexual in adult life, had some episode of homosexual experience in their school years. Fifty years ago such a revelation about an individual would have been considered certain evidence of total depravity.

Nathan Leopold, aged nineteen, and Richard Loeb, aged eighteen, were members of cultured and influential Chicago families. Their fathers were multimillionaire businessmen, as was the father of Robert Franks, their victim. They lived in an elite residential section of Chicago, the Loebs across the street from the Franks, the Leopolds a few blocks away.

The two young men, known to their families as "Babe" (Leopold) and "Dicky" (Loeb), had been brought up in luxury, adored by their parents and siblings, and admired for their intellectual attainments. Both were postgraduate students at the University of Chicago—Loeb in history and Leopold in law. Leopold, who also spoke and read fifteen languages and was an ornithologist of professional standing, had just passed exams for transfer to Harvard Law School in the fall. He had been the youngest graduate in the history of the University of Chicago; Loeb was the youngest to graduate from his college, the University of Michigan. They considered themselves exceptional teen-agers as indeed they were. Their friendship was intense and each played a distinct role: Loeb was the leader; Leopold the follower.

On May 21, 1924, these two extraordinarily gifted young men killed fourteen-year-old "Bobby" Franks and then demanded ten thousand dollars ransom from his father with the promise of his safe return. Their motive for the crime, as they later testified, was the experience of committing a murder. The ransom demand, they explained, was thought up "to add interest" to the crime.

The kidnap and murder had been planned in every detail. First Loeb registered in a Chicago hotel under the assumed name of Morton Ballard. He deposited a suitcase in the room and established residence. Next Leopold, posing as a salesman from out of town, rented a car. He selected one the same model, age, and color as the car he owned so that if people who knew him saw him driving they would notice nothing odd. The agency required a reference from someone in Chicago, and he gave the name of Morton Ballard. A phone call to the hotel reached Loeb, who testified to the reliability of the car renter.

The ransom note had been written in advance and carefully typed. It began "Dear Sir," because the boys had not yet selected a victim. It must be someone who would be physically easy to overpower and from a family that could come up with the ransom, but since this was to be the perfect crime there could be no telltale motive for the killing. They must avoid selecting someone they disliked, had fought with, or had a grudge against. It was all to be completely arbitrary with the victim chosen the day the deed was to be done. They had, however, considered the young grandson of Sears Roebuck president Julius Rosenwald—Loeb's father was vice-president of the corporation—and Loeb had even once suggested his own younger brother!

Late in the afternoon on May 21 they drove near an exclusive private school, which Loeb himself had attended, located a few blocks from his home. They watched the boys coming out the door and first picked a ten-year-old who was walking with a teacher. They watched and followed him but he went off down a side street with a group of other boys. They waited. At about five thirty they spotted the Franks boy, who was walking home from school after umpiring a baseball game in the school playground. He was a small boy—about five feet tall—who frequently played tennis with Loeb on the Loebs' private court. Leopold drew up to the curb and Loeb called out to Bobby, offering him a lift home. When the boy declined—his house was only two blocks away—Loeb said that he wanted to talk to him about a new tennis racquet. Bobby jumped into the car and a few minutes later, while his partner in crime drove down the busy daylit street, Loeb hit the child on the head several times with a heavy chisel, pushed him down on the rear floor of the car, and stuffed his mouth with rags. He was dead almost instantly.

There were still many hours until dark and they cruised around passing the time until they could unload the body. At one point they parked the car, left the dead boy in the rear under a bloodstained blanket, and went into a restaurant for dinner. When darkness came they drove to a swampy area south of the city, stripped the body to halt identification, poured acid on the face which they mistakenly thought would destroy the features, and placed the corpse inside a large pipe at a railroad culvert. Leopold knew the spot because he often led bird-watching classes in the area. They then buried the victim's shoes and belt nearby, took the rest of his clothing to burn in the Loeb furnace, drove home, and posted the ransom note, which they had addressed to Mr. Franks. The next morning they washed bloodstains from the car and returned it to the rental agency.

Although the murderers had expected that the body would not be found for months and perhaps never, a man on his way to work the next morning spotted a foot protruding from the end of the pipe and called police. Meanwhile, the ransom note was received at the victim's home. It told the frantic parents, who had notified the police the night before of Bobby's failure to arrive home from school, that their boy was well and would be returned by the kidnappers upon receipt of ten thousand dollars. They were instructed to go to the bank and take out the money: two thousand dollars in twenty-dollar bills and eight thousand dollars in fifty-dollar bills, all bills to be old and unmarked. The money was to be put in a large cigar box and then wrapped in paper and sealed. A call would come in the afternoon telling them where the ransom would be collected.

When police asked the Franks to come by and look at the body of a boy answering the description of their son, Mr. Franks was so convinced of the sincerity of the ransom note that he refused to go. His brother-in-law went in his place. At 1 P.M. a phone call notified Mr. Franks that he was to proceed with the money to a drugstore where he would receive further instructions. The distraught father failed to note down the address and as he was trying to recall the location he received another call informing him that the body found in the culvert was that of his son.

The unfulfilled part of the plan reads like one of the detective stories which inspired it. Had Mr. Franks gone to the pharmacy he would have found a note directing him to board an Illinois Central train with the money. He would then have been directed to go to the last car in the train and look for further instructions which Loeb had placed in the timetable receptacle. This note would order him to stand on the train's rear platform and throw the money box off at a very specific point outside Evanston.

The youthful killers were not seriously dismayed by the fact that the body had been found and the ransom was not thrown from the train. They read the details in the press with great excitement. The case provided front-page news from the beginning, and when the body was identified the Chicago police chief immediately ordered "a general roundup of all persons suspected of being degenerates." Rewards were offered by Mr. Franks and the *Chicago Tribune* for clues leading to the detection of the murderer. A search was made through Bobby's school for the typewriter, identified as an Underwood portable, on which the ransom note had been written. Four instructors in the school who were found to be in financial distress were held for questioning, and their names were blared out in all the newspapers. Bizarre and disturbed people who bore no actual guilt in the case broke into the scene. A large wreath at Bobby Franks' funeral was found to have a note saying "Sympathy of George Johnson"—the name used by the kidnapper when he telephoned Mr. Franks. The florist described the purchaser as blond and thirty to thirty-five years old. The day after the funeral the bereaved parents received a note reading: "You dirty skunk. Your daughter will be next."

Another man unconnected with the crime wrote a letter confessing to the murder and announcing that he was going to commit suicide. Soon afterward a depressed middle-aged clerk made a suicide attempt. His room and pockets were filled with clippings about the case.

Leopold and Loeb were fascinated. They bought all the papers as they hit the stands and read every word. Leopold had a busy week. His brother had just become engaged and there was a round of parties. He also had several dates with a girl friend and made further plans for his trip to Europe, which was to begin in two weeks. The steamship tickets had been purchased and his father had given him three thousand dollars to cover his summer expenses abroad. He had no problem enjoying all this diversion despite the fact that headlines announced that a pair of horn-rimmed glasses had been discovered near the body and were assumed to belong to the killer. He realized at once that they belonged to him.

The fact that the glasses soon led the police to the proper culprits was ironic and unlikely. For a murderer to drop his glasses by the corpse when committing a "perfect crime" was ridiculous, particularly in this instance since Leopold had no idea they were in his pocket at the time. They had been prescribed several months before when he was suffering from headaches. The correction was very minor and when the headaches disappeared he stopped wearing the glasses, leaving them in an old jacket which he donned the day of the murder. When he read about the clue in the newspapers he searched his room, drawers, and pockets and found they were missing. He was unconcerned, however, since he assured himself and Loeb that they were the most common lenses and frames imaginable. Furthermore, if they *were* traced to him he had a perfect alibi. He had brought bird-watching classes to the very spot a week before the murder, had taken a clumsy fall right near the culvert rushing to photograph a bird, and could allege that he must have dropped them at that time. Members of the class would remember the incident.

A week passed. Police stepped up their efforts to find a sixteen-year-old girl who had disappeared from home the same week. Was a multiple child murderer on the loose? The girl was found living with a stable boy. She told police she hated school. That day Nathan Leopold took his girl friend out in a canoe and he played the ukelele while she read aloud from a book of French poetry.

The next day, as he was getting ready to take a class of children on a bird walk, the maid announced that two police officers were in the library and wished to see him. He was brought to the police station where four other new suspects were also being questioned. The glasses were not so commonplace after all. They had a very new patented hinge connecting the ear piece to the frame, which was sold by only one shop in town. The shop had issued only three pairs of these frames with his prescription. One pair went to a man who had been abroad for several months; the other to a woman who came to headquarters wearing hers; the third pair was sold to Leopold.

The suspect was urbane and relaxed. He told police that he was an "advanced thinker" and an atheist—and the owner of the glasses. He explained how he had tripped during the bird walk and, at their request, he took flop after flop with the glasses in his pocket. They stayed firmly tucked in place. He was asked the make of his typewriter and he said it was a Hammond. They checked and it was so. When they asked where he had been the evening of the crime he sheepishly admitted to having been out driving and drinking with his friend Richard Loeb and two prostitutes. The boys had concocted this alibi together in advance. How could the police ever expect to locate two girls who had been picked up on a street corner and who called themselves Agnes and Mary?

Loeb was brought in for questioning. He was delighted to assist the police and pointed out, as a detective-story fan, some clues they really should follow up. His story of the night with Agnes and Mary wasn't much like Leopold's, but police didn't really expect teen-agers to tell the truth about that sort of adventure. The young men's parents had no doubt whatsoever about their innocence but they stated, as did their sons, that they should be held until completely cleared.

Actually, the police didn't find the two bright and wealthy teen-agers very likely suspects. They treated them with great respect. Why, after all, would these boys need ten thousand dollars? A teacher at the school with a wife, young children, and a mortgage and perhaps some gambling debts seemed more the type they were looking for.

And then, with the very best of intentions, the devoted Leopold family chauffeur came in to save Babe. He knew the murderers must have had a car and Leopold owned his own car, but the chauffeur suddenly realized he could prove him innocent because he knew the car had not been taken from the garage that day. He himself had tinkered with it and brought it to a repair shop later and he could prove the date because on the way he bought some pills for his wife and the date was on the bottle!

The police were very interested in the story. Without his car how had Leopold picked up Agnes and Mary? Despite the shaky alibi they were about to release both suspects because of insufficient evidence connecting them with the crime. They decided to question them independently just a bit longer. To everyone's surprise, each boy blurted out his confession. Leopold described the location in a swamp where he had disposed of the Underwood typewriter, and it was recovered. The killers described the crime and their attempt to collect ransom in considerable detail. Within hours the newspapers had the story.

The confessions agreed in all details except that both boys accused each other of actually striking the death blows. Loeb later explained that he lied "to spare Mopsie's [his mother's] feelings." (Leopold's mother had died when he was seventeen.) In a legal sense it made no difference which of the boys did the actual killing—their guilt in the matter was equal. State's Attorney John Crowe announced that he had "a perfect hanging case" and there seemed to be little question that he was right. There were two capital crimes in Illinois at the time. One was murder and the other, a decade before the Lindbergh Act, was kidnapping for ransom. Richard Loeb and Nathan Leopold had committed both offenses.

The youthful culprits chatted willingly with reporters, who noted every arrogant and unsympathetic word. One wrote that Leopold described the murder as "an experiment," comparing it to the way a scientist might pin an insect. Both boys seemed to believe that their intellectual superiority raised them above the rules which govern society. Neither showed any remorse, nor did they indicate that they feared the death penalty. Although they had not expected to be caught, the possibility of capital punishment had obviously not deterred them from the crime. In fact, both fantasized about being hanged. Leopold stated that if the sentence were death he would first write a book giving his philosophy to the world. He would then list seven universal questions and attempt through spiritualism to answer them from the grave. Psychiatrists retained by the state's attorney at the time of the inquest did not find them insane. They called them "smart alecks" and Crowe announced that being a smart aleck was not sufficient reason for a murderer to escape the gallows.

The issue of the wealth of both families was widely discussed. When famed attorney Clarence Darrow was hired to defend the case the state's attorney's office sent out the statement: "The fathers of these boys have an estimated combined fortune of 15 million dollars, and we suppose it will be these millions versus the death penalty." Both families countered with assurances that they had no intention of going to extraordinary lengths in the defense of their sons and that they had no wish to defeat justice. If the boys were mentally deranged they felt that society should be permanently protected from any possible menace they might pose in the future. Mr. Darrow's fee, they said, would be set by the Chicago Bar Association. Psychiatrists called to testify would receive whatever payment was standard.

To Darrow, then sixty-seven years old, the notorious case was one more opportunity to put forth his views in opposition to capital punishment. Never in his long career had anyone he defended been sentenced to execution. Never had he faced such pressure for the extreme penalty. He was to say of the Leopold-Loeb trial that he had never witnessed "so much enthusiasm for the death penalty as I have seen here. It's been discussed as a holiday, like a day at the races."

To the astonishment of the court, the press, and the public, Darrow entered a plea of guilty on behalf of his clients. A plea of not guilty (by reason of insanity) would have called for a jury trial. The defendants had been so thor-

*Nathan Leopold (l.) and Richard Loeb (r.) committed "The Crime of the Century" when they killed fourteen-year-old Bobby Franks simply for the thrill.*

oughly denounced as "fiends" and "monsters" and the clamor for their execution was already so great that it would probably have been impossible to find a single juror who was not in a hanging mood. A plea of guilty entitled defendants to a hearing on the sentence before a judge.

The *Chicago Tribune* announced that they were considering broadcasting the proceedings on the radio. A public-opinion poll voted them down. Everyone feared that other teenagers would be morbidly fascinated and perhaps influenced by the case.

The prosecuting attorney made an opening statement: "The state is going to prove not only that these boys are guilty, but that they are absolutely sane and should be hanged." He added, "In the name of the people of the State of Illinois and the parenthood and childhood of the state, we demand the death penalty for both of these cold-blooded and vicious murderers." He proceeded, as though the plea had been not guilty, to build up a great mass of evidence verifying all the facts of the crime and the guilt of the defendants.

Darrow's defense was constructed entirely on the testimony of psychiatrists. He contended that, although he did not believe the boys to be insane, they were "mentally diseased." Since the court must hear any evidence "in mitigation of the punishment," such evidence was being presented in a plea for a sentence of life imprisonment rather than a sentence of death.

Under psychiatric examination the two partners in crime emerged as very different personalities. In the judgment of the doctors, Loeb had genuine criminalistic tendencies. He was the "mastermind" who dreamed of murder, plotted and planned, read endless tales of crime and detection, and even delighted in visions of being caught and jailed and admired by the public as the greatest criminal of all time. In discussing the killing he told psychiatrists that as he hit Bobby Franks with the chisel, "I got great excitement, great heart beating, which was pleasant. I was cool and self-possessed. I had quite a time quieting down Leopold."

Leopold's reaction to the murder was different. "He bled," he told the doctors. "I said, 'This is terrible. This is terrible.' Loeb laughed and joked." Leopold was described as a "mental slave" who would never have initiated the crime but whose infatuation with Loeb was so great that he was unable to resist the pressure to join in the act. In his own book, *Life Plus 99 Years*, written thirty-four years later, the remorseful middle-aged man could explain only that he joined in the crime "to please Dick. His friendship was necessary to me." Leopold enjoyed fantasies in which he was abused and played the slave, doing whatever was demanded of him by his king. His king was Richard Loeb whom he had described to friends as "the most wonderful man in the world."

Despite their intense friendship it was disclosed that each boy had thought of killing the other. It was felt by psychiatrists, however, that neither could have functioned alone, that it was the combination of their personalities that made the murder of the Franks boy possible.

Psychiatrists pointed out that both Loeb and Leopold had missed essential developmental experiences common to most boys and girls in their teens. They had been adoringly tended by governesses, walked to school every day, babied and pampered—and then suddenly thrown into the company of much older boys when they entered college at fourteen. Both took up drinking very young and Loeb was censured several times by his fraternity brothers for excessive indulgence. Their college friends, who were brought in to testify, found them odd. Loeb seemed to them childlike and erratic, endlessly argumentative. He delighted in picking pockets and later committed other thefts. Leopold was arrogant and abrasive, snobbish and strange. Because of the whispered testimony about their sexual development a misunderstanding arose and many in the courtroom had the impression that there had been some sexual molestation of the victim, Bobby Franks. There was absolutely no evidence of such a thing and the judge found it necessary to emphasize this point.

Dr. William White of the country's largest mental hospital, St. Elizabeth's in Washington, D. C., found that although the two young men had grown physically and intellectually, they had remained extremely retarded morally and emotionally. Loeb, found to be aged four to five emotionally, was the more severe case. Leopold scored only slightly higher with an emotional age of up to seven. Neither boy showed remorse about the crime and reporters noted their high spirits during the trial. Loeb wrote cheery notes to his parents assuring them that "I am really not in the least despondent." A representative of the Ku Klux Klan left another sort of note at the Loeb home. It said, "If the court don't hang them we will. K.K.K."

An enormous mob fought to hear Darrow's closing summation on August 22. His speech was long and eloquent. In great detail he spoke of the senselessness of the crime and demonstrated that it could only have been conceived by diseased minds. He spoke of the fine homes in which the boys lived. He spoke of their brilliance and promise and their constructive plans for the future—and the fact that they threw all this away for a "thrill." He spoke of the incredible stupidity of this "perfect crime"—the fact that Loeb left his library card and book in the suitcase in the hotel; the fact that the crime was perpetrated in daylight in their own neighborhood. He spoke of the way they drove the corpse down populous streets past the homes of people they knew. He reminded the judge that they parked the bloodstained car in front of Leopold's house, cleaned it the next day in his garage, risked detection at every step. Is this the way normal minds work? he asked.

Darrow, who claimed to have saved 102 prisoners from hanging, then spoke out against the death penalty. "We are asking this court to save their lives, which is the least and the most that a judge can do," he said. "You may stand them upon the trapdoor of the scaffold, and choke them to death, but the act will be infinitely more cold-blooded, whether justified or not, than any act that these boys have committed or can commit. . . . For God's sake, are we crazy?" he asked. "In the face of history, of every line of philosophy, against the teaching of every religionist and seer and prophet the world has ever given us, we are still doing what our barbaric ancestors did when they came out of the caves and the woods. . . . I am pleading for life, understanding, charity, kindness, and the infinite mercy that considers all. I am pleading that we overcome cruelty with indebtedness, and hatred with love. I know the future is on my side . . . I am pleading for the future. I am pleading for a time when hatred and cruelty will not control the hearts of men, when we can learn by reason and judgment and understanding and faith that all life is worth saving, and that mercy is the highest attribute of man."

He expressed his view that life imprisonment might be a more extreme punishment than death. "I hate to say it in their presence, but what is there to look forward to? I do not know but that Your Honor would be merciful if you tied a rope around their necks and let them die." Leopold was to remember these words all his life and to contemplate suicide several times.

When Darrow finished his speech many in the courtroom were in tears, including the previously cool-tempered defendants. The decision from Judge Caverly came three weeks later. The sentence was life imprisonment for murder and ninety-nine years for kidnapping with ransom. He said that in coming to his decision his main concern had been the age of the defendants and the fact that only two minors had ever been executed in the state of Illinois. He was acting, he said, "in accordance with the progress of criminal law all over the world and the dictates of enlightened humanity."

The decision dispelled all talk of money and influence. A minor, according to the judge, was a minor. The case rested on the facts on their birth certificates. The psychiatric testimony had not officially determined the sentence, but its implications for future cases and new definitions of legal responsibility were far-reaching. A month later Darrow publicly debated the subject "Is Capital Punishment a Wise Policy?" with a noted New York judge, striking additional points for the abolitionist cause. The following summer he would become even more famous for his defense of Thomas Scopes and the teaching of Darwinism in the so-called "monkey trial."

In September, 1924, reporters followed the teen-agers as they entered the Illinois State Penitentiary at Joliet to begin serving their sentences. They lingered inside the prison gates, describing the pampered rich boys in their prison garb and gleefully quoting a fellow prisoner who said the two had been a little too "ritzy" when they arrived but that now they had come "down to earth" and were accepted into prison baseball games as regular guys. For several years afterward their birthdays were noted in the newspapers—along with the observation that they would not be eating cake on the occasion.

In 1936, Richard Loeb, aged thirty, was killed by a fellow convict. The news was spread across the front page of major newspapers, along with reports of the death of King George V of England. Loeb had been savagely slashed fifty-six times by a man serving a term for larceny. The razor had been stolen from the prison barber shop and the assailant claimed that Loeb made aggressive homosexual advances, but there were no witnesses and the facts are not certain. Leopold's long prison record was devoid of any incidents of homosexuality, a point later emphasized in his parole hearings.

Before his death Loeb had made a significant contribution. He and Leopold, after a number of years of separation, were brought together again in the new Illinois prison, Stateville. Leopold had been working with illiterates in the prison school, which helped convicts attain education up to the equivalent of eighth grade. Together, in 1933, he and Loeb started the Stateville Correspondence School, a program of high-school level courses which they conceived, planned, designed, and taught. By 1940 the school had inmate-students from twenty institutions in other states. Leopold was in charge of languages and mathematics; Loeb had the authority in English and history. Loeb wrote a grammar book for the first English course using as examples sentences drawn from situations in prison life. It was widely praised by educators and has been used by thousands of convicts.

Nathan Leopold became a model prisoner and an extremely valuable human being. Remorse for his crime, which descended upon him almost ten years later, threatened to destroy his sanity. He made a conscious commitment to atone by serving others. When a convict who had been blinded during a holdup came to the prison, Leopold learned Braille so that he might teach him to read. He learned the hand language of deaf mutes some years later.

He took over the prison library and built a few shelves of books into a professionally catalogued sixteen-thousand-volume collection. After soaring through three correspondence courses in higher mathematics through the home study program of the University of Iowa he qualified himself to outline mathematics courses for prisoners. Graduates of the Stateville Correspondence School who were later paroled were able to apply for decent jobs. Several others went on to colleges which accepted their accreditation from the prison school. A book for parolees named *A New Day and How to Make It* was written by Leopold early in his prison years and became a standard. All through his decades in the penitentiary he wrote business and personal letters for less capable fellow convicts, framed their requests for clemency and for rehearings by parole boards. He worked in the prison's Sociological Research Office and did a thorough study of the predictability of parole success which appeared under a pseudonym in *The Journal of Criminal Law and Criminology*.

During his years in prison this remarkably intelligent man continued his self-education and eventually became fluent in twenty-seven languages. He talked with convicts of every nationality and in many cases assisted second generation Americans in learning the language of their parents.

One of Leopold's greatest contributions was in the World War II Malaria Project. His inquiring mind had led him to an interest in medicine. When the necessity arose for volunteer human "guinea pigs" Leopold, then working as an X-ray technician in the hospital, was among the first to apply. He was given one of the most virulent strains of malaria and new drugs were tested on him which were later used to cure soldiers who had contracted the disease.

As a result of Leopold's work in the project, the governor

of Illinois, Adlai Stevenson, reduced his sentence from ninety-nine to eighty-five years so that he might become eligible for parole earlier. At the time of his trial not even Darrow had recommended parole but by the 1950's the world had changed and it appeared to all who knew him that Nathan Leopold was an entirely different man as well. However, the current state's attorney presented himself and made a speech saying Leopold should have been executed in 1924. Parole was denied. At the time of his first parole hearing he was forty-eight years old, had been in prison since the age of nineteen, and was considered by many authorities to be the most striking example known of total rehabilitation.

Soon afterward a sensational novel about a thrill killing was published in which fact and fiction were inextricably mixed. It was called *Compulsion* and it was based on the murder of Bobby Franks. The novel was an immense success and became a best seller. The names of Loeb and Leopold were changed in the book but were liberally used in promotion. The book was made into a play and also a movie. Leopold felt that this new publicity was not only unwelcome but harmful to his chances for parole. He successfully sued the author, Meyer Levin, and the film producer, Darryl Zanuck, for invading his "right of privacy." He also, in 1957, granted his first magazine interview—to *Life* magazine—which presented him without sensationalism as the man he had become. Photographs showed a slightly potbellied, balding, middle-aged man in prison garb somberly going about his work in the hospital and library.

If Nathan Leopold had been the only example of a life prisoner who made extraordinary contributions to society, the story of his rehabilitation would have significance only for Leopold himself and the people he directly helped. Instead, his story is singular only as the most famous of a number of remarkable cases.

Another fascinating example is Robert Stroud, who became known in the 1950's when he was the subject of a book called *The Birdman of Alcatraz*. The account, by Tom Gaddis, a former probation officer, was later made into a film of the same name with Burt Lancaster playing the lead. Stroud went to prison in 1909 at the age of nineteen on a manslaughter conviction which carried a sentence of ten years. In a fit of passion he had killed a man in Alaska who was his rival for a woman's affection. After seven years in Leavenworth Penitentiary in Kansas he became enraged when a guard reported him for breaking the rule of silence at the table. He stabbed the guard with a knife he had managed to conceal, killing him instantly. He was sentenced to death despite the fact that no one had been hanged in the state of Kansas for forty-two years. His mother went to Washington with a petition for executive clemency saying that her son had been insane when he killed the guard. She was granted an interview with Mrs. Woodrow Wilson who passed on the petition to the ailing President. President Wilson commuted Stroud's sentence to life imprisonment. Stroud was to spend the rest of his life in jail. He was provocative and unremorseful and because of the nature of his crime and his belligerent personality he spent an unparalleled forty-three of his fifty-four prison years in solitary confinement, forbidden to mingle with fellow prisoners or even to walk in the prison yard.

During this period Stroud became compellingly interested in the scientific study of canaries. He built an aviary in his cell and, with books and a microscope donated by Wesleyan University, educated himself in scientific technique. His most famous book, *Stroud's Digest of the Diseases of Birds*, written after two decades of observation and experimentation, was the major work in the field. He supported his mother for decades with the sale of his bird medicines, which were marketed through the mail to owners and breeders. He died in prison in 1963. He had come up for parole numberless times but was never seriously considered eligible.

Nathan Leopold's parole was eventually granted five years after his first hearing. The time was 1958 and Leopold was fifty-three years old. He was a diabetic maintained by daily doses of insulin and he had had several minor heart attacks. Poet Carl Sandburg, who had become interested in the case, traveled to Illinois to testify in favor of his release. When Leopold actually walked through prison gates into a world he hadn't seen for thirty-four years, mobs of photographers and reporters followed him everywhere and made it impossible for him to visit the graves of his parents. He proceeded directly to his new ten-dollar-a-month job at Castañer, a hospital operated by the Church of the Brethren in Puerto Rico, three hours by car from San Juan. Here he found his opportunity to serve in the outside world, free from publicity, accepted simply for himself and for what he had to give. Later he took a master's degree at the University of Puerto Rico and accepted a position there as a mathematics teacher. He met and married a widow of about his own age and when he was released from parole, five years later, he and his wife toured Europe for several weeks. He continued his work until 1971, when he died of heart disease. His obituary was accompanied by pictures of Leopold in his sixties and Leopold at nineteen seated in the courtroom with Darrow and Loeb. It was read with the greatest interest by a world which had not forgotten his crime. He was survived by his widow and two brothers, who had long since changed their name.

The "Crime of the Century" can be viewed today as a triumph for the abolitionist cause. The ghastly murder had been ballyhooed in lurid detail in newspapers in every city in the country. Correspondents from the European press corps relayed the story abroad. It stayed on the front pages daily and repetitiously from the time of the murder until Judge Caverly announced his decision almost four months later. Excerpts from Darrow's address were printed and read by millions, most of whom had decided in advance that the cause of justice demanded their execution. The fact that they were spared the death penalty gave the case its greatest long-range significance and influence. The other half of the story—the almost unbelievably successful rehabilitation of Nathan Leopold—has remained another highly persuasive argument against capital punishment. An inestimable number of people were directly helped by this man, who gave the gift of his adult life to the service of the needy people with whom he lived—his fellow convicts.

# VII

# THE ROSENBERGS

CLARENCE DARROW had predicted in the 1920's that capital punishment would soon be abolished throughout the world, but the history of the death penalty in this country during the next quarter of a century was to be a matter of a few steps forward and a few steps back. Organized groups continued their efforts to reform state and federal legislation. By 1930 five states still had a mandatory death sentence for capital crimes; by 1951 only Vermont and New York still retained such a law. But in the 1930's two abolitionist states—South Dakota and Kansas—reintroduced the death penalty. In 1934 the federal Lindbergh Kidnapping Act broadly extended the scope of capital punishment. During World War II attention was diverted to matters more directly involved in national security, and little publicity attended the ritual executions of murderers and rapists.

It was the Rosenberg case which officially reopened the issue of the death penalty. The execution of the Rosenbergs on the charge of conspiracy to commit espionage remains as the most shocking instance in this century of the discriminatory way in which capital punishment has been imposed in America.

It was 1951, twenty-seven years after the sentencing of Leopold and Loeb, when Judge Irving Kaufman of the United States District Court for the Southern District of New York referred to the espionage case of Julius and Ethel Rosenberg as "The Crime of the Century." His purpose in resurrecting the familiar phrase is unclear although most likely the presiding judge simply meant to emphasize the gravity of the crime of which the Rosenbergs were accused. Certainly, except in the degree of publicity it was accorded, the case of the atomic bomb spies bore no obvious relationship to that of the murderers of Bobby Franks.

Later many people would liken the Rosenberg trial more appropriately to that of Sacco and Vanzetti. But here again there would be comparison problems. Like the Sacco-Vanzetti case that of the Rosenbergs took place in a period of political hysteria, and it is naive to believe that judges and jury members were less affected by this panic than the rest of the population. The enemy was the same in both instances—Soviet Russia. But the Rosenbergs were accused, tried, convicted, and put to death for a specific political crime. Sacco and Vanzetti were judged guilty of murder, although their trial and sentencing were inappropriately influenced by prevailing hostility toward their political affiliations. Today, although their innocence has never really been indisputably established, the crown of martyrdom rests comfortably on shoemaker Nicola Sacco and fish peddler Bartolomeo Vanzetti. It does not become the Rosenbergs. Their memory—Ethel, with the prim mouth and inscrutable expression above the dowdy fur-collared coat, and Julius, a thin dark-eyed man with a tiny mustache—fills many of those who vividly recall the early 1950's with a feeling best described as acute uneasiness.

It is acceptable to weep for Sacco and Vanzetti, but most people in this country believe unhesitatingly that the Rosenbergs were guilty as charged. When they received the sentence of death it was accepted by the American public as a just penalty. A quiet few believed them innocent. Some avoided the issue of guilt and spoke out against the death penalty. Many well-informed critics of the case who have reread all the evidence and reconsidered all questionable testimony and subsequent data have concluded with the perspective of twenty years that the Rosenbergs were guilty of conspiring to commit espionage; that the information they secured and passed on to Russian agents was of questionable value; that their case should have been reviewed by the Supreme Court; that imprisonment was surely warranted; that the infliction of the death penalty was excessive and outrageous—determined not by the enormity of the crime but by the temper of the times.

In 1951 when the Rosenbergs were sentenced to die McCarthyism was approaching its peak and the Korean conflict was raging. The Soviets had exploded a nuclear device and fear of an atomic arms race was at the panic level. Dorothy Thompson, writing for the Washington, D.C., *Evening Star*, questioned whether the Rosenbergs would have received the death penalty if they had been tried during World War II, at the time when their espionage activities were said to have taken place. But few American writers or readers troubled themselves with such distinctions. There was also surprisingly little notice given to the fact that the Soviet Union had, in 1944 and 1945, been our ally, not our enemy.

The result was that the Rosenbergs, parents of two young

children, went to the electric chair sentenced by a judge who accused them not only of participation in espionage activities during World War II but of having caused the Korean War! In the twenty-six legal actions attempted during the two years between their sentencing and their death no superior judiciary saw fit to halt the execution. The Court of Appeals repeatedly upheld the verdict; seven times the Supreme Court denied review. Presidents Truman and Eisenhower refused to grant clemency. After all legal resources were exhausted the Rosenbergs were put to death in New York's Sing Sing Prison on June 18, 1953, the date of their fourteenth wedding anniversary. Since they were Jews and the day was a Friday, the hour of their execution was moved forward from 11 P.M. to 8 P.M. so that they were dead thirteen minutes before sundown. The official decision was to avoid giving offense by violating the Sabbath with the double electrocution.

The chain of discovery which led to the Rosenbergs as key figures in an American atom bomb espionage ring began with nuclear physicist Klaus Fuchs. Fuchs had been a member of a team of British scientists who worked on atom bomb projects in this country during World War II. From December, 1942, until June, 1946, he had been assigned to the top secret research center at Los Alamos, New Mexico. In early 1950 Fuchs was arrested in London and charged with being a Soviet agent. He pleaded guilty and confessed to having obtained secret material both in England and in America which he passed on to the Russians. He received the maximum sentence allowable in Great Britain—fourteen years imprisonment.

Fuchs identified as his intermediary in this country a chemist from Philadelphia named Harry Gold. Gold was arrested by the FBI. He also pleaded guilty and confessed to having served as courier, delivering information regarding national defense secrets between Fuchs and a Soviet vice-consul in New York named Anatoli Yakovlev. He was charged with having met with Fuchs seven times in New York, Massachusetts, and New Mexico during the summer of 1945. The confessions of Fuchs and Gold agreed and Gold received the maximum prison sentence under American espionage law—thirty years.

The Espionage Act of 1917, under which the Rosenbergs and other accomplices were sentenced, was originally enacted to discourage German-born Americans from reverting to old loyalties during World War I. It provided for maximum imprisonment of twenty years if the act was committed in peacetime and the option of capital punishment or a maximum of thirty years if it had occurred in wartime.

When Gold confessed to the FBI he revealed the identity of his accomplices. One of these was a young machinist named David Greenglass, who had been assigned as a G.I. to the Los Alamos project during World War II. Gold stated that he received information from Greenglass about the internal workings of the atom bomb including written descriptions and a sketch of the design of a high explosive lens which was a vital improvement in the type of atomic bomb exploded at Nagasaki.

Greenglass was arrested by the FBI in the twenty-dollar-a-month tenement in New York in which he lived with his wife and two young children. After six hours of questioning he confessed to having passed information acquired while working at Los Alamos to Soviet agents. He told FBI agents that he thought it was wrong that the United States was not sharing information about the bomb with Russia, since the country was our ally at the time. It must be noted that a number of top scientists working at Los Alamos whose intelligence and sophistication dwarfed Greenglass's shared this view. They did not, however, act on their conviction. There was considerable disagreement about the army's strict aura of secrecy about the project. Even Harry Truman, during his three months as Vice-President, knew nothing whatsoever about the goings-on. When he took office in April, 1945, after Roosevelt's death, Secretary of War Henry L. Stimson led him aside after his first cabinet meeting and let him in on the fact that an atom bomb was being readied for action. It was Truman who made the final decision to drop the bomb on Hiroshima a few months later.

When arrested, Greenglass told FBI agents that he had given sketches and descriptions to Harry Gold, whom he identified from a photograph, and that Gold had paid him for the information. He had also handed over other material to his brother-in-law and sister, Julius and Ethel Rosenberg. It was the Rosenbergs, he said, who first approached him and persuaded him to join the espionage ring. He added that they had pressed him for names of other likely recruits among the military and civilian personnel at Los Alamos. Greenglass was also charged with violation of the Espionage Act of 1917. He was not sentenced, however, but was held in Federal Detention Headquarters with bail set at one hundred thousand dollars. Newspaper articles pointed out to readers that by law he could be executed. In fact he had decided to cooperate with the government and as reward for serving as chief witness against the Rosenbergs he would later receive the considerably lesser sentence of fifteen years imprisonment. His wife, who confessed to assisting him in his espionage activities, also testified against the Rosenbergs. She was never brought to trial at all.

Julius Rosenberg was arrested in July, 1950, and his wife, Ethel Greenglass Rosenberg, was taken into custody three weeks later. The couple, aged thirty-two and thirty-four at the time, were parents of two sons, Michael aged eight and Robert aged three. They were living in Knickerbocker Village, a housing development on New York's lower East Side. They were unable to raise bail and they remained in jail until their trial eight months later. Michael and Robert were sent to a Welfare Department children's shelter in the Bronx.

The Rosenbergs had grown up in the slums of New York in the same general area in which they were living at the time of their arrest. They were children of immigrant eastern European Jews who had made the bitter discovery that the streets of the New World were not paved with gold. Ethel's father was an impoverished sewing-machine repairman; Julius's was an indigent tailor. The poverty which surrounded them as children was to continue all their lives.

Both Julius and Ethel had been excellent students. Ethel did so well in school that she skipped several grades, graduating from high school before she was sixteen. She was talented in singing and was praised in her classbook as the school's best actress. There was no possibility of college and after high school she took a six-month stenography course and went to work, turning her income over to her parents to assist in the support of the family. She was active in drama groups in the neighborhood settlement house and earned extra dollars singing in the currently popular amateur-night contests. Busy Ethel also became active as a strike leader and union organizer and a collector of money for left-wing and radical causes. At a New Year's Eve dance being held as a fund-raiser for the International Seamen's Union, Ethel, who had consented to sing, met a college student two years younger than herself named Julius Rosenberg.

Julius Rosenberg had grown up in a tenement a few

blocks away from that in which the Greenglasses lived. His father hoped that he might become a rabbi, but he decided early on a career in engineering. He attended City College, a free institution, and graduated with a degree in electrical engineering soon after his marriage to Ethel Greenglass. He and Ethel were humorless intense young people—unglamorous energetic activists and grindingly poor. Despite their poverty they contributed to many organizations classified as Communist front groups and worked soliciting contributions from others. They attended meetings and sang and spoke at rallies.

Julius's first job was as a civilian engineer with the Army Signal Corps. Starting at a salary of two thousand dollars a year he worked up through gradual raises to three thousands dollars annually. He continued working as an inspector of electronics products until 1945 when he was fired, charged with membership in the Communist party. Thereafter he worked briefly at Emerson Radio Corporation and then opened a small machine shop dealing in surplus equipment with two of Ethel's younger brothers, Bernard and David. David Greenglass had recently been mustered out of the Army.

The shop was a financial disaster and considerable hostility broke out between the Rosenbergs and the Greenglasses. Accusations as to who was responsible for the failure flew back and forth and relations between them deteriorated. When Julius decided to buy out his two partners he was unable or unwilling to repay David one thousand dollars of his original investment. Ruth Greenglass supported her husband fully in his outrage at having been so mistreated by his brother-in-law and a state of alternately cold and hot war existed between the Greenglasses and the Rosenbergs.

It was soon after this that shabby, obscure Julius and

Ethel Rosenberg were named by Greenglass as central figures in the Soviet atomic spy network. Within a year they were world famous.

The trial of the Rosenbergs began on March 6, 1951, in Manhattan's Federal Courthouse at Foley Square. It lasted fourteen days. Tried with the Rosenbergs was a former City College classmate of Julius's named Morton Sobell, who had been indicted as a member of the same espionage ring. He had been returned from Mexico where he had fled with his family after Greenglass's arrest. Greenglass was not tried with Sobell and the Rosenbergs because he had pleaded guilty. Yakovlev, the Russian agent who had also been named in the indictment, had left the country well before this time. The three defendants pleaded not guilty.

Spy prosecutions can take many forms. The Rosenbergs were not accused of committing espionage but of the specific crime of *conspiracy* to commit espionage in wartime. "Conspiring" involves joining together, and in this case, those who were alleged to have conspired had every reason to get together for purely social purposes. Rosenberg, Sobell, and a man named Max Elitcher who was the sole witness against Sobell had been friends and classmates at City College. The Rosenbergs and Greenglasses were relatives. It was no small part of the sordid fascination of the trial that it pitted brother against sister, friend against friend. It was the duty of the prosecution to convince the jury of the reliability of the witnesses against Sobell and the Rosenbergs, who stated that their purposes in meeting were *not* social. The witnesses were also self-confessed accomplices in the spy ring, and the testimony of accomplices is traditionally considered less reliable than that of disinterested parties. It became a matter of deciding whether to believe the story told by the witnesses or that of the defendants. There was little effort made in the press to educate the public on the legal distinction between committing an act and conspiring to do so, and the terms "treason," "espionage," and "conspiracy" were used virtually interchangeably.

Judge Kaufman was forty years old, the youngest federal judge in the country at the time. The indictment charged that starting on June 6, 1944, the Rosenbergs, Sobell, Greenglass, and Yakovlev had conspired together, and with Harry Gold and Ruth Greenglass, with intent to deliver to the USSR information on American national defense secrets, believing that this information would be used to the advantage of the foreign country. When the jury was selected it was made up of ten white men, one black man, and one white woman. Among them were two accountants, a restaurant owner, a tennis club caterer, a bank auditor, an appliance salesman. Several Jews had been summoned but none qualified as jurists. This fact was pointed out by critics of the trial, but it seems unlikely that their presence on the jury would have been particularly sympathetic. Most American Jews felt embarrassed or outraged by the Rosenbergs at the time.

The prosecutor informed the jury that the Rosenbergs had stolen "through David Greenglass this one weapon that might well hold the key to the survival of this nation and mean the peace of the world, the atomic bomb." He referred to the Rosenbergs as traitors who "persuaded David Greenglass, Mrs. Rosenberg's own brother, to play the role of a modern Benedict Arnold while wearing the uniform of the United States Army."

The first witness called was Max Elitcher, an electrical engineer and former member of the Communist party who testified that Sobell and Rosenberg had tried to influence him to pass on classified information and recruit others for espionage work while he was working in Washington with the Navy Bureau of Ordnance. Sobell, he said, was busy secreting classified information from his place of employment at the time, the General Electric plant in Schenectady. On one occasion while in New York he accompanied Sobell, who was delivering a thirty-five-millimeter film can to Rosenberg although he did not know the contents of the can. The very friendly Elitchers and the Sobells had bought houses next to each other and were living there at the time of the trial.

On cross-examination it was brought out that Elitcher, while working for the Navy, had signed a loyalty oath falsely denying membership in the Communist party. He admitted that his fear of being prosecuted for perjury had been a factor in his decision to tell all he knew when approached by the FBI. Along with Ruth Greenglass, Elitcher was never prosecuted.

Next came David Greenglass, the star witness for the prosecution. He testified that while he was serving in the Army in 1944 his wife Ruth had been invited one night to the Rosenbergs' for dinner. Ruth was about to pay a visit to David in New Mexico in celebration of the couple's second wedding anniversary. After the meal Julius and Ethel informed Ruth that David was working on the construction of an atom bomb. They revealed to Ruth that Julius was part of an espionage ring gathering information for the Soviet Union and they told her that they wanted facts about the top secret project from David. They assured Ruth that David would agree that it was a good thing to help our Russian allies. When she went to New Mexico, David was persuaded to reveal the identity of the important scientists who were working on the project under code names. He also described the size of the operation and the design of the buildings and laboratories. Ruth reported to the Rosenbergs on her return and two months later when David was in New York on furlough he wrote out more information and drew sketches for Julius of the high explosive lens mold which was being made in the shop to which he was assigned. He also listed others working at the secret installation whom he deemed likely people for espionage work. Sketches recently made by Greenglass based on his memory of those he drew for Rosenberg six years earlier were produced. He said that Ethel had typed up his handwritten notes, making corrections in his spelling and grammar.

During the same visit to New York Greenglass said that his brother-in-law took an empty Jell-O box and cut one of the panels into two irregularly interlocking halves. He gave one to Greenglass and told him a courier would come to New Mexico for further information and would, as identification, present the other piece of the box. Julius also took David to meet a Russian who wanted to discuss the lens mold with him directly. The unidentified Russian asked a number of highly technical questions, most of which the young machinist was unable to answer.

A few months later Ruth Greenglass took an apartment in Albuquerque to be near her husband and one morning a man appeared at the door and introduced himself with the announcement, "I come from Julius." He then produced the Jell-O box half. The Greenglasses matched it with their own. The courier took information from him and gave David an envelope containing five hundred dollars. A few months later, in September, 1945, David was again in New York and wrote out more facts about the implosion principle of the Nagasaki bomb. Ethel typed his report and Julius boasted to his brother-in-law of the broad range of his espionage activities.

126

When Fuchs was arrested in 1950, Greenglass and Rosenberg had severed their business association in the machine shop. Greenglass alleged on the witness stand that after the arrest Rosenberg told him that the man who had come to see him in New Mexico bearing the Jello-O box piece was Harry Gold, the courier for Fuchs, and suggested that Greenglass leave the country. After Gold's arrest Greenglass, whose wife had recently given birth to the couple's second child, was still in New York and Rosenberg visited him, gave him four thousand dollars, and told him to go to Mexico. Greenglass gave the money to Ruth's sister's husband, who hid it inside a hassock in his living room. It was later used for legal fees after David's arrest.

Ruth Greenglass took the stand and confirmed her husband's testimony. She said that Julius had told her that they would be well taken care of financially and that the money came from the Russians. As to the Rosenbergs, she said the Russians had given them a citation, a table fitted with a microfilming device, and a watch each. She elaborated on Ethel's busy commitment to typing espionage reports.

Harry Gold was the government's next witness. He was brought from the federal penitentiary where he was already serving his thirty-year sentence. He had received his half of the Jell-O box from Anatoli Yakovlev (who had presumably received it from Rosenberg) along with the instructions to introduce himself by saying, "I come from Julius." He had also visited Santa Fe to collect information from Klaus Fuchs on the same visit to New Mexico and had spent a night at a hotel. The prosecution offered as documentary evidence a photocopy of his hotel registration.

On the eleventh day of the trial Elizabeth Bentley took the stand. Miss Bentley was America's talkiest lady spy—a Vassar graduate who had gone on to graduate work at Columbia University and a love affair with a Russian spy named Jacob Golos. After Golos's death she had decided to tell all. The year was 1945, and since then she had related the tale of her spy activities repeatedly to the FBI, women's magazines, and lecture audiences. At the time of the Rosenberg trial she was putting it all into a book. She was on the stand for several hours. The essence of her testimony against the Rosenbergs was that on five or six occasions she had received telephone calls from a person who called himself Julius and had relayed his messages to Golos. The time period was 1942–43, previous to the dates given in the indictment.

Julius and Ethel Rosenberg testified in their own defense, although Morton Sobell did not. They denied all allegations of espionage activity or intent to commit espionage. Julius stated that he had visited with the Sobells and the Greenglasses as charged, but that the purpose had been social. He said that the furnishing Ruth described as having a photographic function was a perfectly ordinary table, purchased for twenty-one dollars from Macy's. Ethel also denied the existence of a microfilming setup. She denied ever having had any knowledge of espionage activity whatsoever and took the Fifth Amendment when asked if she was a member of the Communist party. Both denied having received watches or any other gifts from the Russians. They denied ever having *known* any Russians.

The judge read his charge to the jury, pointing out that proof of the success of a conspiracy can constitute evidence that such a conspiracy existed. "In this case the government claims that the venture was successful as to the atom bomb secret." The prosecutor had summarized the trial by saying: "We know that these conspirators stole the most important scientific secrets ever known to mankind from this country and delivered them to the Soviet Union." Ethel, who was to die for having been present at two conversations about espionage activities and for typing up Greenglass's notes, was described as having "struck the keys, blow by blow, against her country in the interests of the Soviets."

The defense alleged that Greenglass's testimony against the Rosenbergs was motivated by personal malice and was not based on fact. Elitcher, they pointed out, was a self-confessed perjurer. All three, claimed the defense, were innocent. The jury, however, found all three guilty as charged.

Belief in the disastrous results of the Rosenbergs' spy activities was based on the unquestioned assumption that the Russians would never have developed an atom bomb unless someone had stolen the "secret" and handed it over. The Soviet Union had tested a nuclear device in 1949, four years after America dropped the first bomb on Japan. The event marked the end of America's atom bomb monopoly and the beginning of a frantic search for the culprits. In actuality, many of the most influential American scientists had predicted in 1945 that technologically advanced nations should be expected to "invent" the same device within a few years without any assistance whatsoever. The public, however, hearkened to other voices. Among the authorities quoted was the young representative from California, Richard M. Nixon, a member of the House Un-American Activities Committee. He told reporters, "The President says the American people are entitled to know all the facts. I feel the American people are also entitled to know the facts about the espionage ring which was responsible for turning over information on the atom bomb to agents of the Russian government."

When the Rosenbergs were found guilty the public cheered the disclosure that the espionage ring had been cracked. One week later Judge Kaufman announced his sentence. He spoke of the Rosenbergs as "worse than murderers" and went on to elaborate:

> In committing the act of murder, the criminal kills only his victim. The immediate family is brought to grief and when justice is meted out, the chapter is closed. But in your case, I believe your conduct in putting into the hands of the Russians the A-bomb years before our best scientists predicted Russia would perfect the bomb has already caused, in my opinion, the Communist aggression in Korea, with the resultant casualties exceeding 50,000 and who knows but that millions more of innocent people may pay the price of your treason. Indeed, by your betrayal you undoubtedly have altered the course of history to the disadvantage of our country . . . In the light of the circumstances, I feel that I must pass such sentence upon the principals in this diabolical conspiracy to destroy a Godfearing nation, which will demonstrate with finality that this nation's security must remain inviolate; that traffic in military secrets, whether promoted by slavish devotion to a foreign ideology or by a desire for monetary gains must cease . . . for the crime for which you have been convicted, you are hereby sentenced to the punishment of death, and it is ordered . . . you shall be executed according to law.

Morton Sobell received the maximum prison sentence of thirty years since he had been convicted of nonatomic espionage.

Most of the newspapers accepted the verdict without controversy and commended Judge Kaufman. Within a few months the case had been brought to the United States

*Ethel and Julius Rosenberg (opposite page) ride to jail in a police van after being found guilty of conspiracy to commit espionage.*

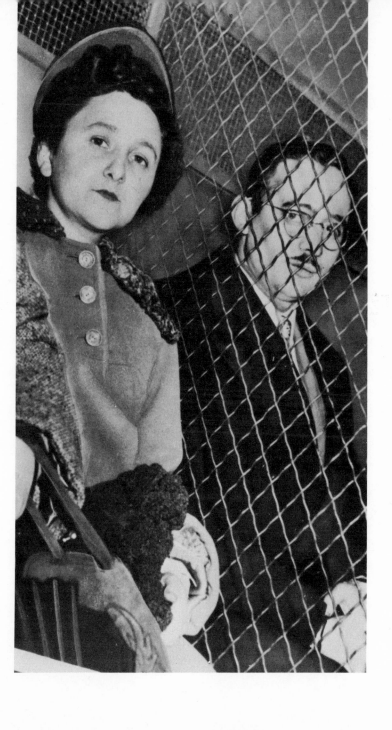

Court of Appeals and upheld. The court passes only on whether or not there have been legal errors in the trial, not on the reliability of witnesses. The defense claimed that Judge Kaufman had not given the defendants a fair trial because of his own prejudice against them. They also stated that the sentence was too harsh. Judge Jerome Frank of the Appeals Court said he had no power to change a sentence.

Ethel was transferred from the Women's House of Detention to Sing Sing's death row and a month later Julius arrived and was put in the men's quarters. Ethel was the only occupant of the women's wing, and was to become the most expensive prisoner in the history of Sing Sing. To fulfill the required maximum security precautions four matrons had to be hired to guard her at all hours.

The couple, who had seen each other only three times in the eight months they spent in jail between their arrest and their trial, were now allowed a one-hour visit a week in the presence of guards. When the children were brought to see them they conferred anxiously by letter in advance about the proper approach. They decided that if Michael asked any questions about electrocution they should calmly assure him that they were not at all alarmed, that the process was totally painless, and that, in any case, they expected the sentence to be altered by an appeal. The boys arrived in good spirits and were taken away screaming at the end of the visit.

Julius and Ethel wrote frequent letters to each other during their confinement. Their correspondence, which makes extraordinarily depressing reading, was collected in a paperback volume titled *Death House Letters*. The book sold for one dollar with all profits going to the children.

The first of a number of articles proclaiming the innocence of the Rosenbergs appeared in a pro-Communist newspaper, the *National Guardian*. The article alleged that Elizabeth Bentley's "Julius" was Klaus Fuchs, whose middle name, Julius, was frequently used by his friends. The Rosenbergs, the article said, were guiltless. The Rosenbergs rejoiced and gained hope for a reprieve.

A Committee to Secure Justice in the Rosenberg Case had been formed. Its membership was made up almost entirely of radicals although some people more accurately described as liberals joined as time went on. After the execution they changed their purpose and their title. They became The Committee to Secure Justice for Morton Sobell.

By the end of 1952, as defense lawyers were framing new motions for appeal, the case had become famous in Europe. "Save-the-Rosenbergs" movements were under way in Belgium, Holland, Switzerland, and England. European intellectuals pointed to the Rosenberg case and the McCarthy hearings and fearfully warned that America was moving toward Fascism. A British physicist named Alan Nunn May, who in most people's opinions had been an infinitely more effective spy than the Rosenbergs, was released from prison after serving seven years of a ten-year sentence. The table around which considerable testimony focused was found in the elderly Mrs. Rosenberg's apartment. It was obviously not equipped for any sort of photographic purposes, but was an ordinary inexpensive item of furniture. A buyer from Macy's confirmed the fact that the store had sold hundreds like it for about twenty dollars.

Also in 1952 a book about Klaus Fuchs and Alan Nunn May reemphasized the fact that the Russians never required the information passed by atomic spies to manufacture the bomb. Nobel Prize nuclear chemist Dr. Harold Urey, who had been listed by the government as a possible witness but had never been called at the trial, wrote a letter to the *New York Times* challenging the conviction and expressing horror at the unequal sentences. The revered Dr. Albert Einstein published notice of his agreement with Urey and sent a letter to President Eisenhower urging mercy. A number of distinguished scientists questioned whether a man of Greenglass's mediocre intelligence—he admitted to having flunked eight out of eight courses in one term at Brooklyn Polytechnic—was capable of having drawn useful diagrams of anything as complex as the atom bomb.

By early 1953 there were picket lines in front of the White House led by Robert and Michael carrying a sign saying SAVE OUR MOMMIE AND DADDY. Michael gave a White House guard a letter he had written to President Eisenhower. It read: "Please let my Mommy and Daddy go and do not let anything happen to them." One motion for appeal called the death sentence "cruel and unusual" because it was unprecedented. Ethel wrote a lengthy plea to President Truman before he left office. Truman stated that "the nature of their crime . . . involves the deliberate betrayal of the entire nation . . . the cause of freedom for which free men are fighting and dying at this very hour." A month later President Eisenhower refused to consider reprieve, blaming the Rosenbergs for the possible "millions of dead whose deaths may be directly attributable to what these spies have done" (in some future nuclear war with the Soviet Union). A petition signed by twenty-three hundred clergymen from twenty-six different denominations asked that he reconsider. He again denied clemency. Forty members of the British Parliament signed a letter to the President warning that the execution might lead to anti-American violence. The British press commented that the President should spare the Rosenbergs for the sole purpose of denying the Communists two new martyrs, and our ambassador in France, Douglas Dillon, expressed the same point of view. When Eisenhower commented publicly on the fact that America and Britain had a common legal heritage a London paper added, "It is a pity that a heritage of clemency is not apparently common to them." Prime Minister Churchill was urged to intercede with Eisenhower and stated that "It is not within my duty or power to interfere." Pleas arrived from Pablo Picasso, from the anti-Communist Pope Pius XII, and from the sister of Bartolomeo Vanzetti. Julius Rosenberg's elderly mother traveled to Washington in an attempt to speak to the President. In front of the White House a news photographer took a picture of two pickets. One had a sign saying: DEATH TO ALL TRAITORS: RID THE U.S. OF RATS. The other said: 3,000 MINISTERS APPEAL TO YOUR CONSCIENCE: CLEMENCY FOR THE ROSENBERGS.

The last legal effort to spare the Rosenbergs took the form of another plea for review by the Supreme Court. It was stated by attorneys that the Atomic Energy Act of 1946 had superseded the Espionage Act of 1917. The new law required that if a sentence of death was to be passed it must be on the recommendation of the jury, not the judge. Two days before the execution Justice Douglas ordered a stay to consider the plea and reconvened the Supreme Court, which had disbanded for the summer. The decision went against the Rosenbergs. Justices Black and Douglas dissented. Justice Frankfurter refused to vote, saying that the rushed conditions allowed no time for careful judicial judgment. His opinion was made public three days after the execution. "To be writing an opinion in a case affecting two lives after the curtain has been rung down on them," he said, "has the appearance of pathetic futility. But history also has its claims."

Until the moment of their executions the promise of a reprieve from death if they would confess hung over the Rosenbergs. They had issued a reply and they remained firm: "By asking us to repudiate the truth of our innocence, the Government admits its own doubts concerning our guilt. We will not help to purify the foul record of a fraudulent conviction and a barbaric sentence. We solemnly declare now and forever more that we will not be coerced, even under pain of death, to bear false witness and to yield up to tyranny our rights as free Americans. . . . If we are executed it will be the murder of innocent people and the shame will be upon the Government of the United States." George Sokolsky wrote for the Hearst papers: "Klaus Fuchs confessed. David Greenglass confessed. Harry Gold confessed. The Rosenbergs remain adamant . . . let them go to the devil."

The Rosenbergs died in the electric chair, maintaining their innocence to the end. The witnesses admired their composure. A telephone line was left open to the execution chamber because there was still expectation of a last-minute confession. Broadway bettors were offering even money on the possibility.

The news of their death was acknowledged with applause on the floor of Congress, where a debate on foreign aid was being held in evening session. Two days later Jean-Paul Sartre wrote in a Paris newspaper that the case was a "legal lynching," and he compared it to the execution of Sacco and Vanzetti. He added, "You believed that the murder of the Rosenbergs was your own private affair . . . but the Rosenberg case is our business. Whenever innocent people are killed it is the business of the whole world. . . . Do not be surprised if we scream from one end of Europe to the other: 'Watch out! America has the rabies. Cut all ties which bind us to her, otherwise we in turn will be bitten and run mad!' "

Americans were shocked and astounded by the furor which took place in Europe over the Rosenberg case. At the time of Sacco and Vanzetti the voice of American liberalism had swelled and grown in united passionate protest. When the Rosenbergs were on trial most American liberals were silent. Thoroughly alarmed by Senator Joseph McCarthy's irresponsible hunt for Communists and "Communist sympathizers," they were reluctant to draw attention to themselves. Many former party sympathizers were totally disillusioned with the policies of the Soviet Union, particularly after the betrayal of Czechoslovakia in 1948. Most people found it difficult to respond to the Rosenbergs, who took the Fifth Amendment repeatedly when queried about their beliefs and affiliations.

In addition, and perhaps most importantly, few Americans saw any reason to distrust the interlocking testimony of the witnesses presented by the prosecution. The American Civil Liberties Union, which had many leaders who were categorically opposed to capital punishment, found that the trial presented no abuse to civil liberties, and they did not officially protest. What, after all, *was* there to protest? Some cried anti-Semitism, but it was constantly pointed out that not only were the defendants Jews but so were the judge, the prosecuting attorney Irving Saypol, and his assistant Roy Cohn, later recruited by the McCarthy Committee. Subsequently a number of books and a Broadway play named *Inquest* attempted to establish the fact that the Rosenbergs were innocent—scapegoats for the Korean War—victims of an FBI frame-up. One by Walter and Miriam Schneir claimed perjury by all major witnesses and suppression of evidence by the FBI.

There is reason to question the trial testimony. The jury had accepted the complete credibility of the witnesses, since there was no "hard" evidence (such as stolen documents) presented. The photocopy of Harry Gold's hotel registration showing he had spent a night in New Mexico could hardly be considered substantially damning evidence against the Rosenbergs. Gold had actually had no contact with Rosenberg, since he took his orders from Yakovlev. David Greenglass, backed up by his wife, was the key witness against the couple and there was reason to distrust his reliability and his motives. Elitcher, who sent Sobell to jail, was already shown to have been a perjurer. On the other hand, the Rosenbergs' innocence was verified only by themselves. It was the fact that the evidence against them from a number of witnesses meshed so well which became persuasive. Many questions might have been put to rest if the Supreme Court had reviewed the case.

If one assumes that the Rosenbergs were guilty, their degree of guilt still seems out of all relationship to the severity of the sentence. As to the harm they caused, the information Greenglass claimed to have given Rosenberg had already been passed on to Soviet agents by Fuchs, who had conveyed other vastly more vital facts as well. The accusation that they caused the Korean War is obviously absurd. The fact that the sentence may have been carried out in revenge for their silence seems obscene.

Julius and Ethel Rosenberg were the only Americans ever executed for espionage by the judgment of a civil court. They were the first people ever executed in peacetime for spying. They were the only people ever put to death under the Espionage Act of 1917. They were the first man-and-wife execution by the federal judiciary. Ethel Rosenberg was the first woman executed under federal law since

Mary Surratt died ninety years earlier because of her complicity in the assassination of Abraham Lincoln.

Morton Sobell, David Greenglass, and Harry Gold are now free men. Sobell served eighteen years of his thirty-year sentence and was released with time off for good behavior. Gold was paroled in 1966. Greenglass returned to his family ten years after the trial.

# VIII
## CARYL CHESSMAN

IN THE YEARS after the Rosenbergs were electrocuted, judges and juries continued to hand down death sentences and a steadily dwindling number of these sentences were ritualistically carried out. Most of the cases involved homicide or rape and capital punishment continued to be viewed as a useful and necessary counterattack to the menace of violent crime.

And then the case of Caryl Chessman became a vivid demonstration of all that is least useful, least reasonable, and most cruel about the death penalty. When Chessman died in San Quentin's gas chamber on May 2, 1960, after having spent twelve years on death row, the moral certainties of many people of good conscience were shaken. The deluge of criticism from citizens of other nations reflected the fact that the case had attracted the same international attention as those of Sacco and Vanzetti, Leopold and Loeb, and the Rosenbergs.

Chessman's delayed punishment set a record. No convict

in American history had spent anything approaching such a length of time awaiting execution. When the matter was concluded his case had become the most litigated proceeding in our criminal law records. There had been doubt about the validity of his trial and doubt about his guilt, but as the years passed these central concerns began to assume less and less importance.

The issue had shifted to whether Chessman, guilty or not, should be executed. It was the same final question that critics had asked about the Rosenberg case, although the background and the circumstances were entirely different. Many people who had approved the sentencing at his trial in 1948 found themselves asking in 1960 precisely *whose* purposes or *what* purposes would now be served by killing Caryl Chessman. Was a man being executed to serve the interests of politicians in California? The idea was too painful to consider and the answer had to be that he was being executed because it *was* just; it was the law. He had been found guilty, condemned to die, and the time—after all this unfortunate delay—had come.

Caryl Whittier Chessman proclaimed his innocence to the end. He was twenty-seven at the time of his conviction; a few weeks short of thirty-nine at his execution. He had, at the time of his death, spent a total of twenty years in jail. He was born on May 27, 1921, in a small town in Michigan, the son of an indigent laborer who was a descendant of the poet, John Greenleaf Whittier. Caryl's middle name honored the distinguished relationship. His mother had been an orphan and she doted on her long-awaited only child. The child, however, was sickly and because of his alarming bouts of pneumonia and asthma his parents moved to southern California. Although he showed outstanding musical ability at an early age, an almost fatal case of encephalitis left him tone deaf and ended his piano playing. When he was eight disaster struck the family. Caryl and his mother and aunt had gone for a ride in a neighbor's car, which was involved in a crash. His aunt was killed and his mother suffered a broken back which left her permanently paralyzed. Caryl was much less seriously injured, but his fractured nose and jaw healed poorly. His nose was permanently humped and crooked, adding a new aspect to the teasing which tormented the puny child. Later it would impel people to describe him as looking "like a tough guy" or "like a thug."

The family was destitute. Chessman's father worked in construction on a movie lot, repaired venetian blinds, and tried a number of other enterprises with consistent lack of success. In the harsh depression years the family went on relief and Mr. Chessman became emotionally disturbed. On two occasions he attempted to commit suicide by putting his head into the oven of the unlit gas stove. Caryl, who was recovering from another serious illness—diphtheria—smelled gas and crawled from his bed to rescue his father as his paralyzed mother lay helpless in the next room.

The skinny child grew to be a tall, strong, clever, and boastful teen-ager ruled by antisocial attitudes which led him to an early career in crime. At first it was a matter of occasionally stealing groceries in the course of his paper route. By the age of sixteen he had been involved in burglaries, forgery, and car theft and was sent to the state's forestry camp, a facility for juvenile first offenders. When he ran away he was moved to a more heavily guarded industrial school.

Unreformed by his "reform" school experiences, Caryl returned to crime almost immediately upon his release. He had decided that people involved in illegal enterprises couldn't complain to the police and he began robbing brothels. His second arrest took place on his seventeenth birthday. After serving his sentence he was paroled and for a short while he worked with his father and spent his free time at home with his invalid mother. Soon, however, he reverted to crime and was caught holding up a filling station and sent to prison as an adult offender charged with armed robbery.

Former San Quentin warden Clinton Duffy first met Chessman at that time and knew him until his death. He included a chapter about the famous prisoner in his book *88 Men and 2 Women.* Duffy, who always found Chessman's brash personality extremely distasteful, recognized him at once as an extraordinarily intelligent man. The twenty-one-year-old convict was selected to become an office clerk and was sent to a course where he learned dictation and typing with remarkable rapidity. Chessman also taught reading to illiterate convicts and edited the prison newspaper in addition to completing his high school equivalency qualifications and taking several college-level correspondence courses. He was a star member of the prison debating team competing with teams from colleges and universities. He wrote scripts for a successful radio program called "San Quentin on the Air." After a few years he so impressed prison officials with his productive activity that he was transferred to a model minimum security prison—and he walked off the grounds and escaped. He was returned to San Quentin soon afterward and then sent to the maximum security facility at Folsom. He remained there until he was paroled in December, 1947. Six weeks later he was picked up by police and charged with the crimes for which he was to die in the gas chamber in 1960.

There had been a series of robberies reported to the Los

Angeles Police Department in January of 1948 which appeared to be the work of the same man. Driving a car with a red spotlight, the bandit had pulled up alongside cars parked in various "lovers' lanes." Many of the victims reported that they had assumed the car was a police vehicle. Some had taken out drivers' licenses or other forms of identification. When they looked up, however, they had seen a man at their car window who held a gun and demanded their money. In two cases, which occurred three nights apart, the gunman had not only robbed but had then taken a woman at gunpoint from her car to his own, which was parked a few feet away. Both women had been forced to commit an act of fellatio. One was returned to her companion after a short interval and the other was driven back to her home.

A composite physical description of the "Red Light Bandit," as he was dubbed, was broadcast to police along with a description of the car. Some victims said the man had worn a handkerchief tied around the lower part of his face. He was described as dark-haired, swarthy, possibly Italian, height five feet six inches to five feet ten inches, weight 150 to 170, age middle twenties. He was said to have a hump on the bridge of his nose, a sharp chin, crooked front teeth, and a scar over the right eye. One man said he had a mustache.

Chessman and another parolee named Knowles were picked up while riding in a car filled with clothing which had just been reported stolen from a men's wear shop. Two policemen in a squad car had been cruising the area searching for a car which matched the description of that used by the Red Light Bandit. They spotted the 1946 Ford club coupe and tried to signal it to stop, but it took off at high speed. After a five-mile chase police caught Chessman and

Knowles, who later insisted that they had tried to escape capture because they were violating parole regulations which prohibit driving a car and associating with other ex-convicts.

Chessman was held in the Hollywood police station for three days of questioning. He firmly denied that he was the Red Light Bandit and he continued to deny it until his death. He readily acknowledged that he was a thief, although he said he was not involved in the robberies cited. He emphatically denied that he was "a sex fiend." He later claimed that police had severely beaten him to force a confession. He also charged that he was threatened because he was about to expose a police-protected gambling setup. The car in which he had been driving was identified as belonging to a Pasadena housewife who had run into a grocery store in early January, leaving the keys in the ignition. It was equipped with a spotlight. Police claimed that Chessman admitted to having covered it with red cellophane when committing the nighttime holdups. Chessman stated that he had agreed to everything they suggested after a long siege of being kicked, punched, and beaten.

Mary Alice Meza, a seventeen-year-old Los Angeles City College student, had been one of the victims. She was sick with an hysterical reaction to her experience. Chessman was taken to her home and when she looked out the window and saw two men—Chessman and a plainclothes policeman—standing by the curb, she pointed out Chessman as the man who had kidnapped and sexually assaulted her.

The other woman, Mrs. Regina Johnson, aged about thirty-five, and her companion of that evening, a man named Jarnigan Lea, identified Chessman at the police station. He was also placed in a lineup with other men, and

145

several people who recently had been robbed identified him. Others viewing the lineup were not able to make an identification. Chessman was brought to trial, charged with a total of eighteen felony counts.

Charles F. Fricke, who presided, was famous for having sentenced more people to death than any judge in the history of the state of California. Chessman had picked up a good bit of legal know-how during his many convictions and he decided that he needed someone better than the public defender assigned to him by the court. His father inquired and found a lawyer who insisted on a retainer fee of fifteen hundred dollars—an impossible sum for the family. Chessman decided, to the intense annoyance of the judge and the prosecutor, that he would conduct his own defense. He agreed to use the public defender, but only in the capacity of advisor on legal procedure. The man whom so many described as "arrogant," "cocky," "a wise guy," confidently went to battle against the formidable bundle of charges.

The jury finally selected was made up of eleven women and one man. Four of the women had daughters who were about the age of the Meza girl, and it is doubtful that an experienced trial lawyer would have let this happen. Chessman had been satisfied to ask prospective jurors whether they had read a recent inflammatory article about his guilt, whether they would weigh the evidence of a policeman more heavily than that of a defendant, whether they felt there was such a thing as a "criminal type."

The defendant was accused of the capital crime of having violated California's Little Lindbergh Law, a statute which permitted the death sentence in cases where a person had been "kidnapped," "seized," or "carried off" for the "purpose of robbery" and had "suffered bodily harm." The law dated from the period of panic after the Lindbergh case when the federal Lindbergh Kidnapping Act became law. California did not have a statute which assigned the death penalty for rape or any other sex crimes.

The most important witnesses at the trial were Mrs. Johnson and Miss Meza. The shock and indignity they had suffered at the hands of the bandit were legally identifiable as "bodily harm." Chessman brought in a number of people who testified that he had been with them on the nights the crimes had occurred. One alibi was provided by his mother, who came to court in a portable bed. Mrs. Chessman, in addition to her paralysis, was suffering from terminal cancer. Another witness was a Mrs. Phillips who said that Caryl, who was to give evidence later of considerable literary skill, often came to help her with a novel she was writing. She remembered that he had been at her house on the day in question because of the relationship of the date to a new plot idea she had evolved. He brought in prisoners from the jail who testified to having seen bruises and abrasions on his body at the time of his arrival, which he claimed were inflicted by police. Police officers took the stand and denied the charge.

Pleading his case, Chessman pointed out numerous inconsistencies to the jury. He admitted to his criminal past but firmly denied involvement in any of the eighteen counts. He denied ever having committed a sex crime and complained that although a psychiatrist had been sent by the prosecution to examine him and determine whether he had the personality of a sex criminal, the doctor had not been brought to court to testify. He pointed out that Mary Alice Meza had emphatically described her attacker as being no more than five feet six inches and that he was six feet tall. He had neither a mustache nor a scar over his right eye and he had never been told he looked Italian. A dentist who had been robbed had said the bandit had crooked front teeth, but Chessman, who had lost his front teeth in a fight, wore precisely even dentures. He asked if it seemed likely that a man with his criminal experience would go to the risk of holding up couples who were carrying five or ten dollars in their wallets.

The prosecutor asked for the death penalty and warned the jurors not to "compromise." He said it was the only "proper punishment" for this "depraved and vicious" criminal. As to the alibis, he accused Chessman of "hiding behind the skirts of a crippled mother." "Do your duty on every count, folks," he said, "particularly those kidnapping counts for the purposes of robbery with bodily injury." The judge warned jurors that if Chessman received a sentence of life imprisonment without parole he could still be a free man some day as a result of executive clemency or a change in the law.

The jury found Chessman guilty of seventeen of the eighteen charges including violation of the Little Lindbergh Act in the cases of Regina Johnson and Mary Alice Meza. They sentenced him to death. The judge added sentences for the fifteen noncapital convictions of from five years up to life imprisonment without parole.

During the next twelve years Chessman fought his sentence through every possible legal avenue. He brought his appeal twice to the Superior Court of Marin County, eleven times to the Supreme Court of California, seven times to the United States District Court for the Northern District of California, five times to the United States Court of Appeals for the Ninth Circuit, and sixteen times to the United States Supreme Court. On eight occasions execution dates were set and eight times stays of execution came in time to permit him to make a further appeal. Then the ninth date was set and Chessman told a writer named William Woodfield, who was investigating the case, "Nothing will save me this time. This is my ninth life. Not even I have more lives than a cat." He was right.

The legal maneuvers began when the court reporter who had taken down the record of the trial died shortly after the trial was concluded. At the time of his death he had transcribed from his shorthand notes less than one-third of the trial testimony. The law requires that the record of the case be transcribed by the man who took the notes, who must then certify his transcription as being correct. Chessman moved for a new trial on these grounds but Judge Fricke denied the motion. Several experienced members of the Los Angeles Superior Court Reporters Association tried to decipher the reporter's notes and found large portions of testimony totally unreadable because the elderly man used an obsolete form of notation and was ill at the time, which impaired his facility. The judge, however, assigned the job to the uncle of the prosecutor's wife, who transcribed 1,194 pages of notes and received ten thousand dollars—ten times the usual fee. Chessman read the completed transcript and claimed it was filled with inaccuracies in the reporting of the testimony, the objections he had made, and the statements of the prosecutor and the judge. His complaint was upheld by the public defender who had served as his advisor at the trial.

One of Chessman's most important points was that the judge had given the jury the impression that the death sentence was mandatory if the defendant was found guilty. Despite his objections the transcript was accepted by the court and the case then went on to an appeal which is automatically required in California when a death sentence has been imposed. Chessman lost the appeal.

The first stay of execution was granted so that Chessman could take the case to the United States Superior Court and years of litigation followed in which the accuracy of the transcript was attacked. Fraser—the court reporter who had been assigned the job of the transcription—was found to be a chronic alcoholic who had been thrown out of court several times by enraged judges. He had shown the rough draft of his transcription to the prosecutor and the judge, who had made "corrections" and "alterations." Chessman had not been permitted to see this draft.

Execution dates were set and then stayed. Chessman acquired three dedicated professional legal assistants, one of whom rode into the woods on a burro to find a vacationing State Supreme Court justice, who then wrote out a stay of execution leaning the document up against a tree trunk. In 1957 the United States Supreme Court decided that Chessman had indeed been denied due process of law for nine years. They ordered that a hearing be held on the issue of the transcript and the case was sent back to Fricke's court. Each side was permitted two experts. Fraser confessed that he had omitted hundreds of symbols which he wasn't able to read, skipping as many as eight full lines at a time. He had also added his own words, saying that in some places it "didn't make sense" unless he did so. He altered some notes on the judge's statements, explaining that he didn't think the judge really meant what he'd said! The experts brought by Chessman attacked the transcript as wildly inaccurate. The prosecution witnesses offered supplementary changes. The motion for a new trial was again denied. The transcript was altered by the addition of literally two thousand corrections—and then accepted.

By this time Chessman was famous. He had written a book entitled *Cell 2455, Death Row*. It was to be the first of three written by Chessman from cell 2455. In his introduction he said:

> I feel impelled to add that the book has been written for one purpose only—because its author is both haunted and angered by the knowledge that his society needlessly persists in confounding itself in dealing with the monstrous twin problems of what to do about crime and what to do with criminals. Pled, consequently, is the cause of the criminally damned and doomed. It's time their voice was heard. And understood.

The eloquent autobiographical tale was an instant best seller. It was translated into more than a dozen languages and over five hundred thousand copies were sold. A film based on the book was also a hit. A growing chorus of voices swelled from around the world opposing Chessman's execution. SPARE CHESSMAN clubs were formed in countries as distant in geography as Brazil, New Zealand, and Sweden. The American Civil Liberties Union, Quaker Friends committees, Mrs. Eleanor Roosevelt, Aldous Huxley, the official Vatican newspaper, the queen mother of Belgium, a handful of glamorous film stars, and hundreds of thousands of ordinary citizens of many lands made their voices heard.

In answer most California newspapers stepped up their campaign for execution. There were constant references to the fact that Chessman had driven Mary Alice Meza mad. This unfortunate girl had been mentally ill from the age of twelve and was diagnosed as the victim of a "chronic schizophrenic process." Two years after her encounter with the Red Light Bandit she was committed to a state mental hospital. Psychiatrists stated that this would have occurred even without her alarming experience. Nonetheless, Miss Meza's mother attended all hearings, announcing to reporters that her daughter would get well if Chessman was hanged. No one noted that, even had this been so, the law does not provide the death penalty for the crime of driving a young woman mad.

Chessman's seventh execution date came due in October, 1959. Governor Edmund Brown denied clemency, saying he must uphold the laws of the state of California. Chessman's lawyers continued to work for a new trial and achieved another sixty-day stay. They claimed that the botched transcript had denied him the equal rights and protection guaranteed in the Constitution when his case went to its automatic appeal. They also opposed the sentence on the grounds that the law had changed. In 1957 the Little Lindbergh Law had been amended in such a way that it could not possibly have been used to convict a man on the grounds on which Chessman had been sentenced. They also protested the "cruel and unusual punishment" of keeping a man on death row for twelve years. Chessman had lived a third of his life under sentence of death, locked into a stone-walled cell four and one-half feet wide (less than the span of his arms outstretched) and ten and one-half feet long (less than twice the length of his body). He had written of this confinement in his book *The Face of Justice*, saying that if he were to be executed and to wake up in Hell, "The Prince of Darkness will be taxed to devise a torture I would regard as more than merely an annoyance after my conditioning by the sovereign state of California." During his stay on the row he had known more than one hundred prisoners who had been taken off to the gas chamber.

The pleas and writs and motions continued. Chessman sat in his cell studying law—he said he had read or scanned ten thousand law books—writing his books, preparing legal papers. The sound of his typewriter was heard day and night, even as his life drew toward its end. It became apparent that many people who demanded his execution had little understanding of the facts of the case. Letters to the governor referred to Chessman as a "murderer," as "the worst criminal in the history of the state." Actually, the acts of which he had been accused are lamentably frequent crimes in our large cities. The *Los Angeles Times* reported that "one atrocious and clever criminal has called into question our judicial system and brought discredit to our laws." It became apparent that Chessman's death was required as a justification of the law, although his lawyers felt that even under the original wording of the Little Lindbergh statute he had been illegally sentenced. The law said that the kidnapping must be "for the purpose of robbery," whereas the robbery in both cases had preceded the kidnapping, which was presumably done for the purpose of sexual assault. The laws regarding sodomy and rape were clearly stated in the criminal code and they did not permit a sentence of death. Chessman fumed with frustration when one of his neighbors on death row who had been convicted under the same law received a commutation. The governor had said that, although there was no doubt about the man's guilt, he had decided that the fact that the criminal was black and the victim white had influenced the jury's decision to sentence him to death rather than imprisonment.

Chessman's eighth execution date was set for 10 A.M. on February 18, 1960. All possibilities for legal action seemed closed and Chessman said good-bye to his attorneys, rewrote his will, and sealed some final letters. He asked to be cremated and buried in Forest Lawn Cemetery with his parents, who had died a decade earlier. Just before midnight on the 17th, a sixty-day reprieve came through from the governor's mansion. Governor Brown had received an

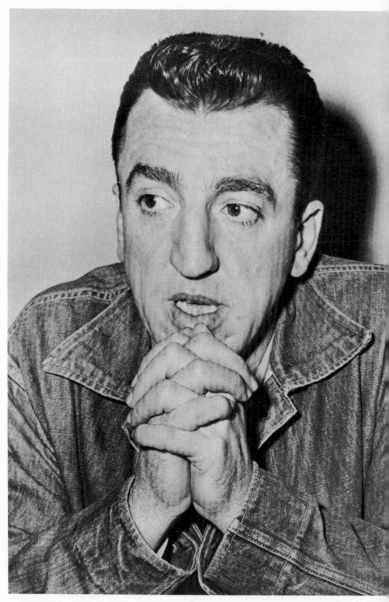

*One week before his execution Caryl Chessman met the press in San Quentin Prison's death row visiting room.*

urgent plea from the State Department asking that he temporarily stay the execution. President Eisenhower was about to embark on a trip to Uruguay, where there was considerable sympathy for Chessman. Word had come from Montevideo that the execution of Chessman might set off demonstrations which would disturb and possibly endanger the President. Brown, who was a sincere advocate of abolition of the death penalty, took the opportunity to "ask the people of California, through the legislature, to express themselves once more on capital punishment." He presented a new bill for abolition to the California legislature for consideration during Chessman's stay. He also temporarily stayed the execution of all the current residents of death row.

Brown, the former California attorney general, had run for governor in 1958 on a platform which included a recommendation that the death penalty be outlawed. A case which resulted in execution three years earlier had been a major influence in his attitude. It concerned a prisoner, named Barbara Graham, who was accused of bludgeoning a woman to death in the course of a robbery attempt. An alleged male accomplice turned state's evidence and accused Barbara of actually doing the killing. Like Chessman, she had a criminal past. She confessed to having been guilty of vagrancy, bad-check passing and prostitution. Like Chessman, she insisted on her innocence of the charge for which she was to die. Reporters photographed her tearfully kissing her eighteen-month-old child who was brought to visit her on death row. As she was entering the chamber with the stethoscope attached to her chest a stay of execution delayed her death. An hour later the stay was canceled and she walked once more to the gas chamber. A film about her ordeal, entitled *I Want to Live*, implied that she was innocent and her conviction remains highly disputable. Brown had said of the Graham case, "This whole business has been one of the most distasteful episodes in California history. It has been like some dark memory out of the Roman Colosseum."

Brown's sincere hatred of the death penalty cannot be doubted, but when his new bill was handed to the legislature the result was chaos. Representatives of both parties were outraged that the governor would bring up the incendiary issue in an election year. One hundred and twenty seats were to be contested in November. There was talk of impeaching Brown. He was blasted in the newspapers and in the mail reaching his office. Politicians agreed that the governor had "passed the buck" to the legislature, where sentiment was thought to be four to one against Chessman.

Chessman wrote a letter to Governor Brown. In speaking of his relationship to the other death row inmates the famous prisoner said, "Somehow they sensed their fate was tied to mine, and mine to a pressing social issue of far greater significance than what might individually or collectively happen to any or all of us."

The political climate was so hostile that in the end the bill was submitted to the Senate rather than to the more liberal House of Representatives, where it was predictably disposed of in the Judiciary Committee which voted eight to seven against. On seven occasions the state's House of Representatives had approved abolition bills, which had then died in the Senate. At the committee hearing on the bill Warden Duffy spoke out from his vast experience against the death penalty, saying that it did not serve as a deterrent to crime. A district attorney agreed, but added that the purpose was not to serve as deterrent but "to punish the evil and reward the good."

When the bill was voted down people of various persuasions applauded. Many advocates of abolition felt that public pressure in the state for Chessman's execution was the greatest hindrance to the abolition of the death penalty. They feared that Chessman must be the sacrifice—that his death would open the way for California to join the abolitionist states.

Chessman's ninth execution date was set for May 2. Petitions with hundreds of thousands of signatures were sent to Brown from abroad, but Brown had promised that if the bill didn't pass Chessman would be "executed under the law." An article in the *Sydney* (Australia) *Sun* said, "Hardly anything can equal the cynicism which could reprieve Chessman two months ago for political reasons but allow him to die when those reasons no longer exist." "It will be a disgrace to America," a British newspaper warned. A member of Parliament wrote, "If you execute Chessman in the end, you won't be executing the man who committed Chessman's crimes. He's a different human personality altogether. You might just as well take a passerby off the street and execute him to vindicate the law." Those who believed in Chessman's genuine rehabilitation remembered his own words in *Cell 2455, Death Row:*

> The long years lived in this crucible called Death Row have carried me beyond bitterness, beyond hate, beyond savage animal violence. Death Row has compelled me to study as I have never studied before, to accept disciplines I would never have accepted otherwise, and to gain a penetrating insight into all phases of this problem of crime that I am determined to translate into worthwhile contributions toward ultimate solution of that problem. This book is a beginning contribution; I would like to believe that it also signals the beginning for me of a journey back from outer darkness.

Preparations for the final event were stepped up. *Life* magazine ran a full-page photograph of telephone company employees stringing up a long line of temporary phones at the prison for the use of reporters assigned to the execution. On the morning of Chessman's death his attorneys presented a new petition to Federal Judge Louis E. Goodman. The judge read part of the plea and then asked his secretary to call San Quentin and delay the execution for at least half an hour while he read further. It was a few minutes before the scheduled time of 10 A.M. Chessman had admitted to a guard on the way to the gas chamber, "Inside of me I had a feeling that the court would relent and let me live." Now he was being strapped into the chair in front of sixty official witnesses. In one of the most ironic endings of any true story in history, the secretary dialed the wrong number and waited while no one answered. By the time the error was recognized and corrected it was a few minutes after 10. The assistant warden answered a telephone, which had been kept open near the execution chamber in anticipation of just such a possibility. "The pellets have been dropped," he shouted into the telephone. "It's too late."

Most of the speculation which followed about whether Chessman could have been spared was pessimistic, but a few students of the case thought he might have lived. It is important to recognize that in the course of twelve years all the battles fought by and for him were on points of procedure. The facts leading to his conviction were never reexamined. The red light crimes started when he was released from prison on parole; they ended with his arrest; he had been identified by several victims and his guilt seemed evident. Many, however, believed him innocent. Since there was sufficient legal doubt about the conduct of the trial to delay his execution for twelve years and sufficient dissatisfaction to alter the law under which he was convicted, these facts alone would seem sufficient to have altered his sentence to life imprisonment. But it was the wrong time, the wrong place.

To many people Chessman was simply and exasperatingly the ultimate poor sport. He had lost and he wouldn't admit it; he had done wrong and been condemned and he refused to take his punishment like a man; he had suffered the mental torture of surviving eight execution dates but it was—after all—his own doing. He was accused of playing with the law, staging tricks on the American judicial system.

The case attracted international attention, however, because for many others Caryl Chessman—who came to trial as a probable psychopath, a nobody from the slums, an arrogant and egotistical career hoodlum—evolved over the years of his ordeal into a symbol of the fight to end capital punishment in America. In his unflagging twelve-year effort to escape execution he also became an object of grudging admiration—an underdog struggling against impossible odds, a man pitting the full resources of a powerful intellect against the system which demanded his death. After his death one more act of malice was reported. Officials at Forest Lawn refused his ashes.

Those who expected his death to lead to abolition of capital punishment in California had a while to wait. In 1972, four months before the Supreme Court came to the same conclusion, California became the first *state* to declare capital punishment unconstitutional, reprieving 107 residents of death row, one-sixth of the total number who were soon to be reprieved by the decision of the United States Supreme Court. Both the California case and the Supreme Court case were argued by Anthony Amsterdam, a brilliant young

159

legal activist and professor at Stanford University Law School.

Caryl Chessman's death was the last "big" execution. It was after this that popular pressure against the death penalty continued to mount without letup. It is not at all necessary to like Chessman or to minimize his criminal career to believe that he should not have been put to death. A Stanford University speaker at a rally soon after his death said, "The real issue is whether even a man who acts like a rat should be treated like a rat or whether, because we, the rest of us, are men, we are bound to treat him like a man." It *is* necessary to ask whether the suffering of his victims was assuaged by his death twelve years later. It is also necessary to ask if executing Chessman was in any way useful to society —if legally killing *anyone* can ever be justified again.

# IX
# THE CASE AGAINST CAPITAL PUNISHMENT

SUPREME COURT JUSTICE BRENNAN, seeking to define "cruel and unusual punishment" in the light of today's humanistic values, wrote, "It is a denial of human dignity for the State arbitrarily to subject a person to an unusually severe punishment that society has indicated it does not regard as acceptable and that cannot be shown to serve any penal purpose more effectively than a significantly less drastic punishment."

Ramsey Clark, former attorney general, said in his book *Crime in America*, "Our emotions may cry for vengeance in the wake of a horrible crime, but we know that killing the criminal cannot undo the crime, will not prevent similar crimes by others, does not benefit the victim, destroys human life and brutalizes society. If we are to still violence, we must cherish life. Executions cheapen life."

Since Cesare Beccaria wrote in the eighteenth century that the threat of capital punishment does not deter men from committing crimes, concerned abolitionists have echoed his words. In recent decades they have been able to cite the results of statistical studies to back up their opinions. And yet lay citizens of every social, educational, and economic class have smugly persisted in the belief that the threat of loss of life—the most extreme punishment society can inflict—is our only sure safeguard against rampant violence. The Rosenbergs were executed for espionage and Chessman for kidnapping, but most executions in this century have been punishment for murder. As Americans applaud improved prison facilities for the restraint and rehabilitation of "less dangerous" criminals they remain dubious about the possibility of rehabilitating murderers and quake at the likelihood of their eventual parole. It seems safer all around to invoke the ancient "justice" of a life for a life; it seems prudent to demonstrate the dreadful consequences of violent crime to would-be offenders. Around the country husbands and wives read of homicide in their morning paper and agree over bacon and eggs that the brute who did the deed deserves to get the chair. They would be astounded to learn that capital punishment has become the least common penalty for murder; that the great majority of all experts who have concerned themselves with the question opposes capital punishment; that murderers are usually first offenders and are the least likely of all felons to repeat their crime; that they make the most cooperative and reliable prisoners; that no relationship has ever been demonstrated between crime rate and the retention of capital punishment, and that the cost to the taxpayer of executing an offender exceeds that of imprisoning him for life.

The most common argument for the retention of capital punishment is that it is, in some primitive or biblical sense, just. There has been considerable debate between clerics on this question and illustrative quotations can be plucked from both the Old and New Testaments to support either the "vengeance" or "mercy" side of the argument. The fact is that a zest for revenge can be aroused in *most* individuals —and then justified by references to reason, righteousness, or Leviticus. *No one* is suggesting that we should literally, in the twentieth century, base our laws directly on our interpretation of Scripture. What we must decide is whether the state should be guided by the same primitive vindictiveness that often rules the opinions of individual citizens.

The point of view of those who wish to see the death penalty retained is usually expressed by people officially involved in law enforcement. One of the staunchest opponents of abolition in this country was the late J. Edgar Hoover, director of the Federal Bureau of Investigation. Throughout his long professional career he supported the death penalty as "proper punishment." He wrote, in the *F.B.I. Law Enforcement Bulletin*, "The professional law enforcement officer is convinced from experience that the hardened criminal has been and is deterred from killing based on the prospect of the death penalty."

Philosophy professor Sidney Hook would like to see the death penalty retained for offenders who, having been sentenced to prison, then murder again. He fears that otherwise a certain percentage of murderers, knowing that they will not be executed, are likely to repeat their crime. He would also favor a law permitting those who elect the death penalty, rather than life imprisonment, to be executed. Another famous academician, Jacques Barzun, wrote in *The American Scholar*, "I happen to think that if a person of adult body has not been endowed with adequate controls against irrationally taking the life of another, that person must be judicially, painlessly, regretfully killed before that mindless body's horrible automation repeats."

Others who advocate retention of the death penalty distrust the statistical evidence that it does not serve as a deterrent to crime. Many feel that such laws assure that young people grow up recognizing that certain crimes are so repugnant that society simply will not tolerate the continued existence of the perpetrator. Retentionists fear the parole of capital offenders and see the death penalty as the only guarantee that they will not commit further crimes and influence others to do so. They ask why the murderer should receive more merciful treatment than that which he inflicted on his victims. Some retentionists hold that the death penalty is more humane than life imprisonment. Few prisoners agree.

To most retentionists the death penalty is "good riddance." They feel morally prepared to decide that the country is better off with*out* such people as Charles Manson and Sirhan Sirhan—both of whom were reprieved with the abolition of the death penalty. In 1966 Truman Capote's book, *In Cold Blood*, became the most moving and humane treatment extant of the "good riddance" theory of justice. Capote minutely detailed the story of Dick Hickock and Perry Smith—two former convicts who wantonly murdered a Kansas wheat farmer and his innocent, attractive family. Capote visited the death house two hundred times for talks with the killers and finally saw them hanged, wept at their passing, and bought their gravestones.

Meticulous surveys have been conducted by penologists and social scientists in an attempt to relate murder to the death penalty. Since we have retentionist states, abolitionist states, and states which have experimented with both, we should be able to associate the status of the death penalty with the prevalance of murder, the top-ranking capital crime. If the death penalty restrains people from committing murder we should find that abolitionist states have a higher homicide rate than states which have retained capital punishment. We should also find that when a state drops the death penalty the murder rate increases. The facts do not conform to these theories. Colorado abolished the death penalty in 1897 and reenacted it in 1901. In the five years before abolition the average number of convictions for murder per year was 16.3. During the period of abolition it did rise—to 18. After the death penalty was reinstituted it *again* increased. Apparently other factors were causing the crime rate to go up. Similar findings were noted when Iowa abolished and then restored capital punishment. The highest number of executions in this country has taken place in the southern states—where we also find the highest number of murders. Rhode Island, which abolished capital punishment in 1852, has a slightly lower number of murders than its retentionist neighbor Connecticut. So does Wisconsin (abolitionist for almost a century) compared to Illinois (retentionist). Both have higher rates than Michigan, which was the first state to abolish the death penalty for murder. The New England states—several of these are abolitionist— have the lowest execution rate and also the lowest murder rate in the country.

A professor of criminal law testified before Congress, during hearings on a bill to abolish capital punishment for federal crimes, saying that after the Lindbergh kidnapping, when so many states elevated the offense to capital status, kidnapping increased in frequency and occurred as frequently in death penalty jurisdictions as in others.

Statistics fail to tell us that the threat of capital punishment reduces the number of murders, but what do the murderers themselves say? Clinton T. Duffy, the former warden of San Quentin, asked each of his condemned prisoners if he or she had thought about the possibility of execution before committing the crime. Most answered that they never expected to be caught; none admitted to having felt the slightest concern about the penalty. Duffy, who spent his entire life in prison work, is a firm opponent of capital punishment. He has stated that he and other men who have worked professionally at the prison know not only that capital punishment fails to deter crime but that "there are more homicides following an execution than preceding same."

Further evidence has demonstrated that most murders are "crimes of passion" in which the killer attacks a spouse, relative, or acquaintance in an unreasoning frenzy of hate, jealousy, frustration, or revenge. Many of these crimes are committed under the influence of alcohol. A high percentage of the murderers are mentally deranged. The death penalty does not loom as an alarming threat to such irrational people.

Tragic instances of murders committed by men intimately familiar with the facts of execution are frequently cited in this regard. A convict ironically named Charles Justice was mechanically inclined and while in prison designed special straps which were an improvement on those being used on the electric chair. His invention was adopted, but soon after his release he committed a murder. He died in the chair, bound with the effective restraints he had contributed to the technology of death.

Another case often related in abolitionist literature is that of Detective Sergeant William J. Mulrine, who had been on the Wilmington, Delaware, police force for twenty years and who was an outspoken advocate of the death penalty. Ten days after Delaware reinstated capital punishment Sergeant Mulrine shot and killed his wife.

An early sociologist in nineteenth-century England who was dubious about the deterrent effect of public executions asked condemned men if they had ever witnessed a hanging. Almost all replied that they had. As noted in Chapter II, during the almost three hundred years when pickpocketing was a capital offense in England, pickpockets were invariably found among the crowds at the gallows. As soon as preparations for the hanging became exciting and the audience became absorbed in the show, they went into action. The scene in no way deterred them from committing a capital offense.

A powerful argument against the death penalty has always been the possibility of judicial error resulting in the execution of an innocent man. We will never know the entire story of Sacco and Vanzetti, the Rosenbergs, or Caryl Chessman and many unanswered questions remain. If a man is imprisoned he is technically eligible to have his case reconsidered in the light of new evidence or new law. Execution, however, is irrevocable. It closes all avenues for reconsideration of his case. It denies a prisoner all possibility for rehabilitation. The story of Nathan Leopold is evidence that such rehabilitation can result in a life of usefulness to others. Caryl Chessman was undeniably a different man in 1960 than he had been in 1948.

We do not know how many innocent men have been hanged, gassed, or electrocuted in this country, but we know it has happened. No legal system in history has provided as many safeguards against this possibility as ours, and yet injustice has been done. Guiltless men have been falsely accused, incorrectly identified, sworn against in perjured testimony. Stays of execution have come as a man is being led to the death chamber—and sometimes just after the switch had been pulled or the pellets dropped. Mentally disturbed people have incriminated themselves and accepted punishment for crimes they never committed. (During the lengthy search for the kidnap-murderer of the Lindbergh baby 205 people are said to have confessed to the crime!) Others of limited intelligence or weak will have succumbed under police interrogation and confessed to criminal actions despite their innocence. Human error in identifying suspects is notoriously common. In a Los Angeles study 28 percent of identifications positively made in a police lineup by eyewitnesses to a crime proved, on follow-up, to be incorrect. Most of those accused bore no physical resemblance to the actual culprit. And yet little evidence is as persuasive to a jury as the victim of violence who points to a man in court and screams, "He's the one!"

When an outrageous crime is committed the resultant publicity can arouse public indignation to such a point that it is almost impossible to find jurors who have not decided in advance on the guilt of the accused. Clarence Darrow was well aware of the fact that public opinion would have sent Leopold and Loeb to their death if they had been tried before a jury. In most states, a person who does not approve of the death penalty will not be allowed to sit on the jury in a capital case. Although polls show that about half the people in this country disapprove of the death penalty, a man tried by a jury of "his peers" has no one to argue on his behalf against a sentence of execution.

It is considered to be virtually a guarantee of infallibility that the unanimous vote of a twelve-man jury is required to send a man to the electric chair and that all jurors must be convinced of his guilt "beyond reasonable doubt." Yet errors have occurred. As an additional check, governors or pardon boards are empowered to commute death sentences to life imprisonment in every jurisdiction in this country if any doubt arises after sentencing. Yet even the most rigid advocates of the death penalty know that a possibility of convicting the innocent remains.

In Great Britain a macabre murder case in which a gross miscarriage of justice appears to have occurred became a rallying point for abolitionists. It involved two men—Mr. Evans and Mr. Christie—and a rather large group of women, all of whom had been strangled.

In 1953 police found the remains of six female bodies in the garden and under the floorboards of a seedy tenement house at number 10 Rillington Place in London. A former tenant of the house named John Reginald Halliday Christie confessed to having strangled the victims and buried their corpses. The press dubbed him "The Monster of Rillington Place." He was tried, found guilty, and sentenced to hang. There was an added aspect to the crime which set it apart from more commonplace murders. Christie had also confessed to having killed another former resident of the house, one Mrs. Evans. Unfortunately, her husband, Timothy John Evans, had already been executed.

The case could not have been more bizarre. Evans was a virtually illiterate truck driver of very low intelligence who one day in 1949 contacted police and confessed to the murder of his wife. Although he said he had stuffed the body into a drain, it was found in a wash house behind the house along with the body of Evans's only child. Both had died by strangling and a man's necktie was still in place around the child's neck. Evans later changed his story and alleged that Christie, who lived in the same house, had killed Mrs. Evans while performing an abortion on her. Christie denied any guilt in the matter and became the main witness for the prosecution. Evans's hanging followed an unsuccessful appeal.

Three years after Evans died Christie strangled his own wife and chucked her body under the floorboards. His other victims were prostitutes whom he brought home, strangled, raped, and buried. Police found a collection of their hair swatches, which the murderer kept in a tobacco tin. He was diagnosed as a fetishist and a necrophiliac. He alleged that during the war he had killed twenty-two other women whose bodies he later deposited on bomb sites. Details of the grisly case horrified and fascinated the public. The murder of the Evans child was never fully explained, but belief in Timothy Evans's wrongful conviction and exposure of the efforts of officials to conceal evidence turned the case into a powerful argument against the death penalty, which was abolished in Great Britain in 1965. Evans, who was not in a position to benefit from clemency, was granted a posthumous pardon.

Cases cited in this country by abolitionists concern men who have been executed—such as Sacco and Vanzetti. More commonly, they center on people who have been pardoned in time and saved from death. This is not surprising. Once a man has been executed, attempts by lawyers, relatives, and concerned citizens to prove his innocence usually die with him. Several books—Edwin Borchard's *Convicting the Innocent*, Jerome and Barbara Frank's *Not Guilty*, and Erle Stanley Gardner's *Court of Last Resort*—document a large number of instances in this country in which justice was not done.

One early case was the 1893 conviction in Mississippi of nineteen-year-old Will Purvis. Purvis, who had been sentenced to hang for murder on the evidence of eyewitness testimony, was taken to the gallows, fitted with a noose, and dropped through the trap. The knot slipped and he fell to the ground unharmed. Purvis had declared his innocence up to the moment the trap was sprung. Executions were still public and when the crowd saw the "hanged" man attempt to climb back up on the scaffold with his hands and feet still tied some saw it as a sign of divine intervention. The minister called for a vote from the crowd on whether or not to rehang the criminal and almost all the five thousand people who had come in bloodthirsty enthusiasm to witness a death voted no. The helpless sheriff returned the prisoner to jail, and his sentence was commuted to life imprisonment. He was released after two years when the state's star witness admitted that he was no longer sure Purvis was the correct man. He was entirely cleared of all implication in the murder by another man's deathbed confession many years later. Compensation of five thousand dollars was granted him by the state for his years in prison at hard labor. Many people were reminded of the famous case of "Half-Hanged Smith," a man who had already been dropped through the trap when a messenger galloped up with his reprieve. He was cut down alive and displayed his scarred neck to awed admirers for the rest of his life.

An unlikely occurrence at the gallows saved another innocent man from death in the case of a railroad brakeman named J. B. Brown. A brutal murder had occurred and the public demand that someone be brought to "justice" resulted in hasty conviction of Brown on what turned out to be false evidence. On the day set for his execution he was standing with the noose around his neck as the death warrant was read aloud. To the intense astonishment of everyone present an error had been made or a joke successfully perpetrated and the name of the foreman of the jury was written in on the warrant instead of the name of the prisoner. A postponement was declared and Brown's attorneys brought his case before the governor, who commuted the sentence to life imprisonment. After he had served twelve years new evidence proved that he had not committed the crime and he was granted a full pardon.

There have been a number of "murder" cases in which, after a suspect has been charged, the "victim" has turned up alive and well. In most cases a mysterious disappearance has been followed by the discovery of some unidentifiable bones or a decomposed body and the false assumption has been made that the murder occurred. In 1908 in a small rural all-black community in Virginia the preacher and assistant preacher of the church frequently quarreled. On the day before the preacher disappeared, his assistant, in an argument about church affairs, was heard threatening to kill him. Some time later the decomposed body of a large black male was found in the river wearing a ring very similar to the one owned by the preacher. The assistant preacher was accused of having murdered his superior and, although the prosecutor asked for the death penalty, the jury decided on imprisonment instead. Three years later the preacher was found living just across the state line in North Carolina, where he had absconded with some church funds. The man who had taken on the responsibility of looking for him was the clerk of the circuit court who knew both men well and felt certain that no murder had been committed.

It was also due to the intervention of interested citizens that three young black men convicted of raping a sixteen-year-old white girl were saved from Maryland's gas chamber in the early 1960's and, after six years, pardoned by the governor and released from prison. Two brothers, John and James Giles, and a friend of theirs named Joseph E. Johnson, had been convicted of rape by two separate juries. A citizens' committee was formed after the death sentence was passed, which worked gathering information and funds for

*The most eloquent opponent of the death penalty, Clarence Darrow, is shown in court with his famous defendants, Nathan Leopold and Richard Loeb, seated behind him.*

their defense. They accused the county police and the prosecuting attorney of withholding relevant testimony about the character of the girl, who had earlier been reported to juvenile authorities as being of poor moral character and beyond her parents' control. The accused men had insisted that the girl consented, that she informed them that she had already had intercourse with "sixteen or seventeen boys" that week. The jurors had refused to believe this, but when details of the girl's promiscuous behavior were brought out later the lives of the Giles brothers and Johnson were spared.

A famous murder trial of 1913 involved an unjust conviction and resulted in the lynching of a pencil-factory owner named Leo Frank. Frank had been sentenced to death for murder by a Georgia court but it was later discovered that the real culprit had committed perjury when testifying against him. Frank was a Jew and a great deal of incendiary anti-Semitic sentiment was aroused at the time of the trial. When the governor revoked the death sentence a violent mob kidnapped Frank from prison and hanged the innocent man from a tree. Photos of his dangling corpse and bits of the rope were sold to enthusiastically approving townspeople.

Possibilities for error in sentencing accused offenders to death will remain as long as human beings are fallible. President Lyndon Johnson's Crime Commission pointed up the fact that the excitement aroused when a capital case is being tried "destroys the fact-finding process." Consequently, appellate courts give particularly close scrutiny to cases in which the death penalty has been passed and executions may be stayed for years. Sacco and Vanzetti spent six years awaiting execution. Four decades later Caryl Chessman spent almost twelve. Although these legal precautions reduce the chance of executing the innocent, long waits on death row and repeated delays and stays of execution can be psychologically intolerable to the prisoner. Inmates awaiting execution live in a solitary limbo, unable to socialize with prisoners other than those on the row. They are locked in their cells alone for virtually the entire day and are forbidden to divert themselves with prison work projects. They eat in their cells and spend their brief recreation period in the corridor with other condemned prisoners —talking, playing checkers, or very occasionally viewing a movie. Lights blaze twenty-four hours a day. Razors and eating utensils are carefully collected immediately after use because a constant vigil is maintained to prevent inmates from committing suicide. The stresses of the last days, weeks, and months of the life of a condemned man often do lead to suicide attempts and some are successful. Psychotic breakdowns are also not uncommon. Since the law does not permit execution of an insane man, the prisoner must be treated, returned to health, and *then* executed. A famous case concerned a condemned sex offender named Henry McCracken who deteriorated into a state of genuine insanity as his execution approached. He saw rabbits in his cell, defecated on the floor, babbled incoherently, was unable to respond in any meaningful way to questioning. He was taken from prison to a mental hospital where electric shock was used to restore him to reality. The rabbits disappeared as well as all his other symptoms and he was deemed cured. He became interested in playing the guitar as doctors cheered. He was then returned to death row where electricity—which had been used to cure him—was employed again, this time to kill him. In many instances extensive medical care and major surgery have restored prisoners to the state of health legally required for execution.

The Russian novelist Dostoevski was sentenced to death as a young man and reprieved at the last instant, as he stood facing a firing squad. In his novel *The Idiot* he described the torment of awaiting execution.

> The chief and the worst pain may not be in the bodily suffering but in one's knowing for certain that in an hour,

and then in ten minutes, and then in half a minute, and now at the very moment, the soul will leave the body and that one will cease to be a man and that that's bound to happen; the worst part is that it's certain. When you lay your head down under the knife and hear the knife slide over your head, that quarter of a second is the most terrible of all.

Chessman wrote from the death house about the agonies suffered by a condemned man as did Barbara Graham in a series of letters to a friend. Both expressed the desire to be dead and finished with the intolerable waiting. When the powerful film, *I Want to Live*, was released, French Nobel Prize novelist Albert Camus wrote a review in which he said, "Here is the reality of our time, and we have no right to be ignorant of it. The day will come when such documents will seem to us to refer to prehistoric times, and we shall consider them as unbelievable as we now find it unbelievable that in earlier centuries witches were burned or thieves had their right hands cut off."

Several books written in recent decades by prison wardens vividly portray the horrors of execution—the barbaric physical cruelty which follows the mental cruelty of the wait on death row. Many men who have remained cool and composed all through their maximum security confinement fall apart as execution becomes imminent. Men have been dragged to the gallows in a faint or in a last-minute desperate physical struggle to be free; they have been electrocuted with blood spurting from an artery punctured by a fingernail at the door to the death chamber; they have been gassed screaming, moaning, and shrieking within hearing range of horrified witnesses and other condemned men who await their own execution dates. When a man is electrocuted, prisoners on death row cringe in their cells as the lights dim because of the sudden powerful demand on the building's electric current.

None have returned from the grave to tell the tale and many people believe that hanging, electrocution, and lethal gas are all painless deaths, but those who have witnessed executions have often expressed the conviction that this is not so. It has been suggested that if executions, with all their attendant horror, had been carried out in Grand Central Station or on television capital punishment would have been abandoned in this country long ago—that it is largely *because* we are not exposed to the sight of human beings like ourselves suffering this ultimate cruelty that we can ignore it. Clinton T. Duffy, the former warden of San Quentin Prison, who witnessed over 150 executions and officiated at 90, described death by hanging before a Senate hearing in 1968 on a bill to abolish the death penalty:

Hanging, whether the prisoner is dropped through a trap, after climbing the traditional thirteen steps, or whether he is jerked from the floor after having been strapped, black capped and noosed, is a very gruesome method of execution. . . . The day before an execution the prisoner goes through a harrowing experience of being weighed, measured for length of drop to assure breaking of the neck, the size of the neck, body measurements, etc. When the trap springs he dangles at the end of the rope. There are times when the neck has not been broken and the prisoner strangles to death. His eyes pop almost out of his head, his tongue swells and protrudes from his mouth, his neck may be broken, and the rope many times takes large portions of skin and flesh from the side of the face that the noose is on. He urinates, he defecates, and droppings fall to the floor while witnesses look on, and at almost all executions one or more faint and have to be helped out of the witness room. The prisoner remains dangling from the end of the rope for from eight to fourteen minutes before the doctor, who has climbed up a small ladder and listens to his heart beat with a stethoscope, pronounces him dead. A prison guard stands at the feet of the hanged person and holds the body steady, because during the first few moments there is usually considerable struggling in an effort to breathe.

Duffy has also described death by poison gas, which he considers more humane:

In lethal gas the last preparations are not so grim. Lethal gas executions are a bit less nerve racking on the personnel than other methods, and the family of the condemned prisoner, his loved ones and the friends who claim the body do not go through as much of a harrowing experience when they claim a body that has not been mutilated. . . . The prisoner is dressed in blue jeans and a white shirt. He is accompanied the ten or twelve steps by two officers, quickly strapped in the metal chair, the stethoscope applied, and the door sealed. The warden gives the executioner the signal and, out of sight of the witnesses, the executioner presses the lever that allows the cyanide eggs to mix with the distilled water and sulphuric acid. In a matter of seconds the prisoner is unconscious. At first there is extreme evidence of horror, pain, strangling. The eyes pop, they turn purple, they druel [sic]. It is a horrible sight, witnesses faint. It finally is as though he has gone to sleep.

Another authority, Robert G. Elliott, executioner of 382 men and five women, tells of electrocution in his book, *Agent of Death*. The prisoner is dressed in trousers which have a slit right leg seam to permit attachment of the electrode. He is strapped to the chair and the lever is pulled:

The figure in the chair pitches forward, straining against

the straps. There is a whining cry of the current, and a crackling, sizzling sound. The body turns a vivid red, sparks often shoot from the electrodes. A wisp of white or dull gray smoke may rise from the top of the head and the leg on which the electrode is attached. This is produced by the drying out of the sponge, singed hair, and, despite every effort to prevent it, sometimes burning flesh. An offensive odor is generally present.

Duffy and Elliott, along with James Johnston of Alcatraz, John Ryan, warden of Milan Prison, and Lewis Lawes of Sing Sing, have all spoken out against the death penalty. Elliott, who electrocuted Sacco and Vanzetti, has written, "I do not think that the death penalty is necessary to protect society and I do not believe that it should be inflicted . . . I reached my conclusion after being official executioner for a number of years." Just before his own death he stated, "I hope that the day is not far distant when legal slaying whether by electrocution, hanging, lethal gas, or any other method is outlawed throughout the United States."

The old arguments for the retention of capital punishment are increasingly difficult to uphold. The death penalty cannot be demonstrated to work any more effectively than imprisonment as a deterrent to crime. Further, it is—in both a humane and a constitutional sense—"cruel." It is also in both senses "unusual." When a man is sentenced to die for a crime it is not necessarily because his crime is more abhorrent than that of the man who has been given life imprisonment. Was Chessman's crime more vile than that of Leopold and Loeb? It is instead because he committed it in the wrong state, or at a time when public sentiment was more easily aroused to vengeance than it might have been earlier or later, or because he was tried by a "hanging judge," or because the governor of his state was less inclined to grant clemency than another might have been. In the case of Burton W. Abbott, a man who died in California's gas chamber in 1957, executive clemency arrived a few seconds too late. Unlike Chessman, Abbott had been permanently reprieved from execution. The governor's decision came by telephone as Abbott began to breathe the first fumes of cyanide gas rising from beneath his chair. The case was grotesque and highly controversial. Many maintained that the prisoner, who met death after being accused of the murder of a fourteen-year-old girl, could still have been saved. Prison officials insisted that had they rushed in wearing gas masks in an effort to save Abbott they would have endangered the spectators who sat outside the hermetically sealed chamber viewing the execution through a window. The case pointed up a number of problems including the treacherous uncertainty of last-minute stays of execution and the awesomely irrevocable nature of the punishment itself. Men now alive and released on parole have histories which parallel Abbott's—but their stays of execution arrived a few moments earlier.

Prisoners who have gone to their death rather than to prison have invariably been impoverished people represented by court-appointed attorneys. Sometimes these lawyers have had no previous experience in a capital case. Others may be equally as capable as those privately hired by more affluent criminals, but they do not have funds at their disposal to fully investigate and research all possible aspects of the case. A few dedicated court-appointed attorneys have used personal funds to help pursue a case in which they were certain of their client's innocence. Millions have been spent by socialite murderers and participants in organized crime for investigations, appeals, and thorough exploration of all legal avenues and loopholes for reducing the sentence. The death penalty has without question been discriminatorily applied in this country and Justice Douglas, in his opinion in the Supreme Court case of 1972, stated: "We know that the discretion of judges and juries in imposing the death penalty enables the penalty to be selectively applied, feeding prejudices against the accused if he is poor and despised, poor and lacking in political clout, or if he is a member of a suspect or unpopular minority and saving those who by social position may be in a protected position."

There is no record of any affluent member of our society who was actually put to death for a capital crime.

Former Governor Michael Di Salle of Ohio, who has written and spoken out against capital punishment, wrote that death row prisoners have much in common:

> They are penniless. They have other common denominators—low mental capacity, little or no education, few friends, broken homes—but the fact that they have no money is the principal factor in their being condemned to death. I have never seen a person of means go to the chair. It is the well-heeled gangster, the professional killer who can afford the best legal talent to defend him, who gets off with a lesser sentence. It is the poor, the illiterate, the underprivileged, the member of the minority group—the man who because he is without means is defended by a court-appointed attorney—who becomes society's blood sacrifice.

Blacks have been executed in this country in numbers vastly disproportionate to their representation in the population. Completely accurate national statistics on the death penalty only stretch back to 1930. Statistically, 54.6 percent of all people executed for crime in the United States since then have been black, although Negroes represent only 12 percent of our population. Four hundred and fifty-five men have been executed for rape in this period, and 90 percent of them have been black. In the same interval 49 percent of the over three thousand prisoners executed for murder have been black. Of the very small number of prisoners executed for burglary since 1930, 100 percent were black. Due to complex sociological reasons there is an undeniably higher incidence of crime in the black population than among whites, but the figure is still scandalously out of proportion. It has also been pointed out that, while a great many black men in this country have been executed for raping white women, no white man has ever been executed for raping a black woman. Between 1930 and 1944 the District of Columbia and five states—Louisiana, Mississippi, Oklahoma, Virginia, and West Virginia—executed *only* Negroes for rape.

Men are also discriminated against as opposed to women. Only thirty-two women have been executed in the past four decades, while the number of men is 3,827. All but two of the women were convicted of murder. Ethel Rosenberg was the only female prisoner executed during this period under federal law. It is estimated that men commit approximately five times as many murders as women, but again the number who receive the death penalty is wildly out of statistical relationship. At the time of the Supreme Court decision one death row prisoner of the six hundred was a condemned female murderer.

The Fourteenth Amendment to the Constitution guarantees that no state shall "deprive any person of life, liberty, or property, without due process of law, nor deny to any person within its jurisdiction the equal protection of the laws." The equal protection clause has been found to have been violated by this discriminatory application of the death penalty. The three defendants in the historic 1972 Supreme Court case presented typical death row case histories. All were black, as were the majority of the 600 prisoners awaiting execution (257 white, 329 black, 14 Puerto Rican, American Indian, or Mexican). All three victims were white. Two of the men were convicted of rape and one of murder, the only two crimes represented in the death row roster. Lucious Jackson, Jr., convicted for raping a woman while holding a scissors against her neck, had entered the victim's house after her husband went to work. He was twenty-one years old and had previously been imprisoned for auto theft. When he committed the crime he had escaped from a prison work gang and had been at large for three days. Elmer Branch, who tested borderline in I.Q., had raped an elderly widow after breaking into her home at night and demanding money. He had previously been imprisoned for theft. Neither rape victim had been hospitalized or showed medical or psychiatric signs of permanent damage. William Henry Furman, aged twenty-six, had killed a man by shooting through a closed door in attempting to break into a house during the night. Killings which occur during a felony, such as burglary, are treated by law as first-degree murder even though they are unpremeditated and may be accidental. He was judged to be mildly to moderately retarded with occasional psychotic episodes. Jackson and Furman were from Georgia, which has a high rate of executions and a high rate of capital crime. Branch was from Texas.

No one has proven that Furman, Jackson, and Branch were sentenced to death instead of imprisonment *because* they were black, but based on statistics, their chances of receiving the lesser sentence would have been greatly improved had they been white. Justice Douglas said, "A law that stated that anyone making more than fifty thousand dollars would be exempt from the death penalty would plainly fall, as would a law that in terms said that blacks, those who never went beyond the fifth grade in school, or those who made less than three thousand dollars a year, or those who were unpopular or unstable should be the only people executed. A law, which in the overall view reaches that result in practice has no more sanctity than a law which in terms provides the same."

Capital punishment in this country has not been shown to deter crime. It has been discriminatorily inflicted on three groups of people: the less privileged members of society, blacks, and men. It has not been proven a more effective protection to society than confinement in prison. It may also be stated as fact rather than mere opinion that vengeance is no longer an acceptable basis for law at this stage of civilization. The barbaric cruelty, both mental and physical, of the sentence of death is totally repugnant and inadmissible to humane citizens of today. The possibility of sending even a single man to his death for a crime he didn't commit is, for many people, the most potent argument against capital punishment—a sufficient protest with no further reasons required. What justification remains for advocates of the death penalty to rally in defense of their cause? Only the bill—the outraged taxpayer's claim that he should not be asked to pay for life imprisonment of a man who has violated the basic minimal rules for living in society. Again, he is not aware of the truth of the matter. It has been shown that capital punishment is infinitely more expensive than life imprisonment. The costs of long capital trials, sanity hearings, legal and court fees for appeals which may go on for a decade (Caryl Chessman's appeal cost the state of California half a million dollars) are very much higher than they would be if life imprisonment were the most severe penalty. Add to this the high cost of additional guards for other necessities for the maintenance of death rows' maximum security units and the fact that condemned prisoners, who often spend years awaiting execution, are not able to offset maintenance costs which are often largely met by prison industry programs—and the dollars and cents of the situation becomes obvious.

The Supreme Court case of 1972 was the first time the court had been asked to consider the constitutionality of the death penalty itself. Three previous cases involved constitutional challenges to one method or another of inflicting the penalty. In the case of Wilkerson versus Utah (1878) and in the case of William Kemmler (1890) the court was asked to halt shooting and electrocution by declaring them "cruel and unusual punishment." In both cases the constitutional clause was interpreted to mean that torture and methods of execution involving a lingering or unnecessarily painful death were excluded—but not shooting, which is a common means of execution, or electrocution, which although it was unusual at the time, was instituted because it was intended to be humane. In a third case lawyers tried, in 1947, to halt the execution of Willy Francis, a seventeen-year-old boy from Louisiana, who had been sentenced to death for a murder committed when he was fifteen. His execution had been bungled and he survived an inadequate amount of electrical shock on a malfunctioning chair. Since the obviously cruel punishment of unsuccessful electrocution had been accidental, the court approved a second electrocution saying that the first attempt "did not make the subsequent execution any more cruel in the constitutional sense than any other execution." In none of the three cases did the court consider the idea that execution in itself was constitutionally impermissible. It was not until 1972 that the court was asked to consider this question and their bare majority decision that legal executions are themselves a "cruel and unusual" punishment today seems suddenly long overdue.

Is capital punishment now permanently outlawed in the United States? No one can be completely certain at this date. States have restored capital punishment statutes after having abolished them and there is reason for concern in the fact that the four Burger court members—all Nixon appointees—voted in a block against abolition while the five remaining Warren court justices voted the death penalty down. In the future, with inevitable new appointments to the Burger court, could the constitutional question be reopened?

One day after the Supreme Court decision President Nixon stated in a press conference that he hoped the ruling of the Court did not ban the death penalty for the crimes of hijacking and kidnapping. A recent Senate bill includes the provision of the death penalty for hijacking. In the November, 1972, elections Californians voted in referendum to restore the death penalty by overturning the decision of their own state supreme court which, nine months earlier, had declared capital punishment a violation of the state's Bill of Rights. Although the voters may have the right to change the law in California, they are not empowered to overrule the *federal* Supreme Court decision declaring capital punishment unconstitutional, which pertains to all the states. What California is attempting to do instead is to write new death penalty legislation which will *not* contradict the Supreme Court ruling. Three of the Supreme Court justices said that the result of laws enabling judges and juries to decide between death and imprisonment is the fact that those who are executed are the poor, the ignorant, and members of minority groups. For this reason they found that the death penalty had been imposed discriminatorily and therefore constituted "cruel and unusual punishment." Legislators in California and in Florida, Delaware, Utah, New York, Indiana, and several other states are now talking about framing legislation that will conform to their own interpretation of the decision, which is that the death penalty can be considered legal if it is uniformly applied to all who stand convicted of capital crimes—to black, white, rich, poor, women as well as men. Earlier California law retained the mandatory death penalty for train wrecking, perjury when testifying in a capital case, treason directed against the state, and murder of a prison guard by a prisoner serving a life sentence. Is the state legislature prepared to extend the mandatory death penalty to cover murder and other capital crimes? Would such a law be deemed consistent with the Supreme Court decree?

Many questions trouble abolitionists who bemoan the "weak" decision. However, Douglas B. Lyons, executive director of Citizens Against Legalized Murder, Inc., and a leading national authority on the death penalty, firmly believes that efforts to circumvent the decision by drafting new legislation cannot succeed. "There is no way for a death penalty statute to pass constitutional muster," he states. "The death penalty has been abolished."

Arthur Koestler, in *Reflections on Hanging*, summed up the case against legalized killing in one unforgettable moral judgment: "The gallows is not only a machine of death, but a symbol! It is the symbol of terror, cruelty and irreverence for life—the common denominator of primitive savagery, medieval fanaticism and modern totalitarianism. It stands for everything that mankind must reject if mankind is to survive."

# SUGGESTIONS FOR FURTHER READING

Bedau, Hugo, ed., *The Death Penalty in America*. New York: Doubleday, 1964.

Capote, Truman, *In Cold Blood*. New York: Random House, 1965.
Capote's "nonfiction novel" about an actual mass murder and the men who committed the crime.

Chessman, Caryl W., *Cell 2455, Death Row*. Englewood Cliffs, N.J.: Prentice-Hall, 1960.
Chessman's story of the life of a condemned man.

Darrow, Clarence, *The Story of My Life*. New York: Scribner's, 1932.
The great attorney writes of his most famous cases, including the defense of Leopold and Loeb.

Leopold, Nathan F., *Life Plus 99 Years*. New York: Doubleday, 1958.
Leopold's autobiography beginning the day after the killing.

Prettyman, Barrett, Jr., *Death and the Supreme Court*. New York: Harcourt, Brace and World, 1961.
Six cases of prisoners under sentence of death which were reviewed by the Supreme Court. One of these is Willy Francis (see Chapter IX)—the teen-ager who went to the electric chair twice.

Russell, Francis, *Tragedy in Dedham: The Story of the Sacco-Vanzetti Case*. New York: McGraw-Hill, 1962.
The most interesting of the many books on the case.

Schneir, Walter and Miriam, *Invitation to an Inquest*. New York: Doubleday, 1965.
A detailed reevaluation of the Rosenberg case which was the basis of a Broadway play entitled *Inquest*.

Sellin, Thorsten, ed., *Capital Punishment*. New York: Harper and Row, 1967.
Two anthologies of articles about the death penalty which constitute the best reference on the subject.

# INDEX

# ABOUT THE AUTHOR

Elinor Lander Horwitz was born in New Haven, Connecticut, and was graduated from Smith College. Her marriage to neurosurgeon Norman Horwitz took her to Chevy Chase, Maryland, where they now live with their three children. The Horwitzes are avid collectors of books, Persian miniatures, and Islamic pottery, and Elinor, an amateur sculptor, achieved a claim to immortality when her gargoyle was accepted for the face of the National Cathedral in Washington, D.C.

Professionally, Elinor Lander Horwitz has written for many major national magazines and is a regular feature writer for the Washington, D.C., *Evening Star News*. Her previous books for young people are THE STRANGE STORY OF THE FROG WHO BECAME A PRINCE, THE SOOTHSAYER'S HANDBOOK—A GUIDE TO BAD SIGNS AND GOOD VIBRATIONS, and COMMUNES IN AMERICA—THE PLACE JUST RIGHT.